I0048426

Fundamentals of Management

A Beginner's Handbook

Chintan A. Mahida

CANADIAN
Academic Publishing

2013

Copyright © 2013. Chintan A. Mahida

All rights reserved. This book or any portion thereof may not be reproduced or used in any manner whatsoever without the express written permission of the publisher except for the use of brief quotations in a book review or scholarly journal.

Price : $27.86

First Edition : 2013

ISBN : 978-1-926488-03-5

ISBN Allotment Agency : Library and Archives Canada (Govt. of Canada)

Published & Printed by
Canadian Academic Publishing
81, Woodlot Crescent,
Etobicoke,
Toronto, Ontario, Canada.
Postal Code- M9W 6T3
Phone- +1 (647) 633 9712
http://www.canadapublish.com

ACKNOWLEDGEMENT

I am very grateful to Principal U.D. Patel Sir for giving me opportunity to teach Management to Engineering Students.
As an English Teacher, I was little bit confused whether I will deal with Management or Not. But experience is really enchanting. I really enjoyed a lot in teaching Management.

The book is a fruitful result of college notes-study material prepared for the students of GTU by me. Almost 90% students read it and find it very easy to read and understand. Student's reactions towards my material is a source of inspiration for this book.

I dedicate this book to my all students who have enjoyed my lectures, my notes and made me a teacher of Management instead of a teacher of Communication Skills

- **Chintan Mahida**

CONTENTS

Unit - 1 : Introduction to Management and Organizations

Que : Define 'Management.' State the functions of management. Explain

Management is one of the most imperative and interesting disciplines of business. Management is a wide term and has different meaning at different time and under different situation. *Management is an art of getting work done by different people working in different departments.* Management can be defined as *the process of designing and maintaining an environment in which individuals worked together as a group to accomplice any objectives*. Management *is the proper utilization of resources and people.*

D.J.Clough says, "Management is the art and science of decision making and leadership." George R. Terry defines, *"Management is a process consisting of planning, organizing, actuating and controlling."* Management can also be explained in the word itself *Manage Men Tactfully.*

There are basic five functions of Management :

(1) Planning : Planning is the management function that involves setting of goals and deciding the best method to achieve them. The first step in planning is the selection of goals for the organization. Goals are then established for the subunits of the organizations - its divisions, departments and so on. Programs are established to achieve these goals. The plan must be flexible so that it can be modified due to change in working environment and new information. Planning is a rational and intellectual process prior to the actual operations. The Planning process looks into the future and decides the future course of action. Planning is the function that determines in advances what should be done. It consists of selecting the enterprise objectives, policies, programs, procedures and other means of achieving the objectives. Plans made by top level management may cover periods as long as five or ten years. Planning at the lower level covers much shorter periods.

(2) Organizing : When two or more persons work together towards a common goals, authority and responsibility should be given to them. This is the task of organizing. Organizing is the process of arranging and allocating work, authority and resources among an organization's members so they can achieve the organization goals. Different goals require different structure. A list of activities is to be prepared and activities should be distributed among different department. Organizing is also concerned with building, developing and maintaining of working relationships.

The task of organizing is also known as design of an organizational structure. Organizing is the process of establishing the orderly use of assigning and coordinating tasks. Some important steps of organizing are as below :
  (a) *Review Plans and Objectives*
  (b) *Determine the work activities necessary to accomplish objectives*
  (c) *Classify and group the necessary work activities into manageable units*
  (d) *Assign activities and delegate authority*
  (e) *Design a hierarchy of relationship*

(3) Staffing : Employee is the key factor in any organization. No business enterprise can exist without employees. Staffing is concerned with the proper recruitment and training of the employees. Manager has to work with the human resources department to execute this function. Staffing or Human Resource Management (HRM) is the management function devoted for acquiring, training, apprising and compensating employees. Attracting, developing, rewarding and retaining the people needed to reach organizational goals are the activities that build up the staffing function.

(4) Leading : Leading is also known as "directing" and "motivating". Leading in organization means movement towards objectives. Leading involves directing, influencing and motivating employees to perform essential task. A manager has to be a leader as he directs the whole team towards the completion of the organization goal. Planning and organizing deal with the more abstract aspects of the management process, the activity of leading is very concrete; it involves working directly with people.

(5) Controlling : Controlling is based on comparison of actual post-operative data with planned data. Controlling is aimed at regulating organizational activities so that actual performance meets the expected or predetermined objectives and standards of company. Relationships and time are central to controlling activities. For best controlling, compare the result with standards and take the necessary corrective action. Planning and controlling are so correlated that many a times, they are performed concurrently. Harold Kontz said, *"Planning and controlling are non-separable twins."* Thus Controlling is carried out only after the operations are over. Suppose planned target production is 100 units per day, the actual day ends production is compared with the pre-planned production of 100 units. The day end actual production could be 95 units indicating inefficiency in the form of short fall of 5 units.

Que : Explain Mintzberg's 10 managerial roles. (Roles of Manager)

Henry Mintzberg in his book, "The Nature of Manageiral Work" published in 1973, highlighted the roles of managers in an organization. He conducted a study of five executives , the way they spend their time in the organization. He conducted a study of five executives, the way they spend their time in the organization for serving the organization. He classified three major managerial roles each with sub-classification of ten roles. He classified such roles as under :

Interpersonal Roles	Figurehead	Performs ceremonial and symbolic duties such as greeting visitors , signing legal documents. (An executive is considered as a first person of the section, division, branch or a company. He performs all above duties)
	Leader	Direct and motivate subordinate, training counseling and communicating with subordinates. (As a leader, he leads his division through motivating and encouraging the employees under his span of control)
	Liasion	Maintain information links both inside and outside organization; use mail , phone calls , meetings. (As a Laision, he collects the information of his section and co-ordinates it with other sections of the company.
Informational Roles	Monitor	Seek and receive information, scan periodicals and reports ,maintain personal contacts. (He collects and monitors the information is formal and informal through personal contacts)
	Disseminator	Forward information to other organization members; send memos and reports, make phone calls. (He is authorized to disseminate the information)
	Spokesman	Transmit information to outsiders through speeches, reports and memos. (A Manager is an authorized person to speak to either insiders or outsiders as far as his official jurisdiction is concerned.)
Decisional Roles	Entrepreneur	Initiate improvement projects, identify new ideas. (He has creative ideas)
	Disturbance Handler	Take corrective action during disputes or crises; resolve conflicts among subordinates. (As a head, he can handle disputes within his section or between the sections)
	Resource Allocator	Decide who gets resources , scheduling, budgeting , setting priorities (The corporate team allocates the resources among various divisions of the company)
	Negotiator	Represent department during negotiation of union contract, sales purchases, budgets ; represent departmental interests. (The Manager on behalf of the company negotiates various terms binding as well as benefiting the company.)

Trick : FLL MDS EDRN

Que : Explain types of Managers.

The functions performed by mangers can also be understood by describing different types of management jobs.

(1) Functional Managers : Functional managers supervise the work of employees engaged in specialized activities such as accounting, engineering, information systems, food preparation, marketing, and sales. A functional manager is a manager of specialists and of their support team, such as office assistants.

(2) General Managers : General managers are responsible for the work of several different groups that perform a variety of functions. The job title "Plant General Manager" offers insight into the meaning of general management. Reporting to the plant general manager are various departments engaged in both specialized and generalized work such as manufacturing, engineering, labor relations, quality control, safety, and information systems. Company presidents are general managers. Branch Managers also are general manager if employees from different disciplines report to them.

(3) Administrator : An administrator is typically a manager who works in a public (government) or nonprofit organization, including educational institutions, rather than in a business firm. Managers in all types of educational institutions are referred to as administrators. An employee is not an administrator in the managerial sense unless he or she supervises others.

(4) Entrepreneurs : An entrepreneur is a person who founds and operates an innovative business. Michael H. Morris defines entrepreneurship along three dimensions : innovativeness, risk taking and proactiveness. After the entrepreneur develops the business into something bigger than he or she can handle alone or with the help of only a few people, that person becomes a general manager. Michael Dell started Dell Computers from his dormitory room and He becomes wealthiest man and an entrepreneur in short time.

(5) Small Business Owner : Small-business owners typically invest considerable emotional and physical energy into their firms. Note that entrepreneurs are (or start as) small-business owners, but that the reverse is not necessarily true. You need an innovative idea to fit the strict definition of an entrepreneur. Simply running a franchise that sells sub sandwiches does not make a person an entrepreneur.

(7) Team Leaders : A major development in types of managerial positions during the last 20 years is the emergence of the team leader. A manager in such a position coordinates the work of a small group of people, while acting as facilitator or catalyst. Team leaders are found at several organizational levels, and are sometimes referred to as project managers, program managers, process managers, and task force leader. (**Note : The real answer ends here**)

Extra Points for this answer. You can add this point if you want to add.

When we are talking about types of managers, it is necessary to highlight "Types of Leadership" and "Levels of Management."

(1) Autocratic : An Autocratic style means that the manager makes decisions unilaterally and without much regards for subordinates.

(2) Paternalistic : It is just like autocratic and is also essentially dictatorial ; however decisions take into account the best interests of the employees as well as the business.

(3) Democratic : In a Democratic style, the manager allows the employees to take part in decision-making : therefore everything is agreed by the majority.

(4) Laissez-Faire : In Laissez-faire , the leader's role is peripheral and staff manage their own areas of business. The communication is horizontal. This style can be resulted in poor management.

(5) MBWA : Managing by Walking Around (MBWA) is a classical technique by good managers who are proactive listeners. Listening carefully to employee's suggestions, managers gets real-time information processes and policies that is often left out in formal communication. The manager must maintain his role as coach or counselor not director.

There are three levels of management

(1) Top Level Management consists of president, chairman, vice chairman etc.
(2) Middle Level Management consists of head of all departments.
(3) First Level / Lower Level Management consists of workers and supervisors.

Que : Explain the different styles/types/methods of leadership.

Types of managers are distinguished by the way they manage the activities within company. Management styles are the characteristics ways of making decisions. Different management styles can be employed dependent on the culture of the business, the nature of the task, the nature of the workforce and the personality and skills of the leaders. Robert Tannenbaum and Warren H. Schmidt argued that the style of leadership is dependent upon the prevailing circumstances.

(1) <u>Autocratic Leadership</u> : Autocratic leadership refers to the centralized authority in a top person usually the head of the organization. An Autocratic style means that the manager makes decisions unilaterally and without much regards for subordinates. His decision will reflect the opinions and personality of the manager. Subordinates may become overly dependent upon the leader and more supervision may be needed. In this style, the leader or the head of the organization retains all authorities in his hand.

There are two types of autocratic leaders :
  - (a) The Directive Autocratic makes decisions unilaterally and closely supervises subordinates.
  - (b) The Permissive style makes decisions unilaterally but gives subordinates latitude in carrying out their work.

<u>Advantages</u> : Quick decision-making is possible. Secrecy can be maintained. It ensured effective coordination and discipline.
<u>Disadvantages</u> : It kills creativity of subordinates. In case of weak leader flattery develops. It demoralizes talented people. Sometimes the decisions could immature and whimsical which may affect the organization.

(2) <u>Paternalistic Leadership</u> : It is just like autocratic and is also essentially dictatorial ; however decisions take into account the best interests of the employees as well as the business.

<u>Advantages</u> : The leader explains most decisions to the employees and ensures that their social and leisure needs are always taken care of. Communication is again generally downward but feedback to the management is encouraged to maintain morale.

<u>Disadvantages</u> : Employees once again become dependent on the leader.

(3) <u>Democratic Leadership</u> : In a Democratic style, the manager allows the employees to take part in decision-making : therefore everything is agreed by the majority. Communication gets both directions: Upward and Downward. From business's point of view, job satisfaction and quality of work will improve.

<u>Advantages</u> : It satisfies the ego of the employees and thus boosts up the moral. It develops relations between superior and subordinates. It develops creativity in the subordinates. It eliminates the conflicts between the superior and subordinates.

<u>Disadvantages</u> : This type assumes that subordinates are capable of decision making but sometimes incapable subordinates pretend to participate. It delay the decision making process. It is difficult to maintain the secrecy of the decisions.

(4) <u>Laissez-Faire Leadership</u> : In a Laissez-faire leadership style, the leader's role is peripheral and staff manage their own areas of business. The communication is horizontal. This style can be resulted in poor management. Here, the leader detaches him from the duties of management and because of this, coordination gets disturbed. This style can create highly professional and creative groups

<u>Advantages</u> : The subordinates use their creativity and innovative way of handling a situation. It boosts up the morale of the subordinates.

<u>Disadvantages</u> : This style of leadership assumes that the subordinates are competent to decide in the best interest of the company which may not always be true. As there is no linear relationship in the organization, it breaks effective communication.

(5) <u>MBWA Leadership</u> : Managing by Walking Around (MBWA) is a classical technique by good managers who are proactive listeners. Listening carefully to employees' suggestion, managers gets real-time information processes and policies that is often left out in formal communication channel .The manager must maintain his role as coach or counselor not director. By leaving decision –making responsibilities with the employees, managers can be assured of the fastest possible response time. By walking around, management gets an idea of the level of morale in the organization and can offer help if there is trouble.

Que – What, according to you, are the skills a modern manager will require to run an organization. (Explain management skills)	Que – Explain the principles of management as suggested by Henry Fayol.
	(Trick : DAD UUS RCSO ESIS)
Three different types of skills are identified : (1) Technical Skills (2) Human Skills (3) Conceptual Skills (4) Time Skills (1) Technical Skills : Technical Skills refers to the ability of man to carry out any activity in organization. Technical skills reflect the proficiency and understanding of a specialized job. Technical skills are associated with First or Supervisory Level Management. Managers often develop their technical skills through education or training. The technical skill development is continuous process. (2) Human Skills : Human Skills is also called as interpersonal skills. Human skills is work with others as a team member and as a leader. A manager with effective human skills can communicate properly and motivate them to perform well. Every executive deals with human skills. Every manager should follow the employee centered rather than production centered management. Every manager should recognize and appreciate the feelings and expectations of the people and should strive to meet them in possible manner. (3) Conceptual Skills : Conceptual Skills refers to the ability of man to think and to conceptualize abstract situations. Conceptual skills is very useful for finding problem. In organization, every problem must be solved with conceptual skills. Conceptual Skills is associated with top level management. Conceptual skills also include the ability to analyze a situation, determine the root-cause of any problem and devise an appropriate plan. A manager is supposed to be a strategist rather than a person with a short sighted and selfish consideration. (4) Time Skills : Time Skills is an art of scheduling, budgeting, arranging in organization for effective result. Time management has become crucial in recent years. Time management is perhaps most essential for the peson who owns his or her own business or who runs a business out of the home. An important aspects of time management is planning ahead. In short, First Level Managers require more technical skills and human skills . However conceptual skills are not very essential for the managers at the supervisory level.	(1) DIVISION OF WORK : Work should be divided among individuals and groups to ensure that effort and attention are focused on special portions of the task. (2) AUTHORITY : The concepts of Authority and responsibility are closely related. Authority was defined by Fayol as the right to give orders and the power to exact obedience. Responsibility involves being accountable, and is therefore naturally associated with authority. (3) DISCIPLINE : A successful organization requires the common effort of workers. Penalties should be applied judiciously to encourage this common effort. (4) UNITY OF COMMAND : Workers should receive orders from only one manager. (5) UNITY OF DIRECTION : The entire organization should be moving towards a common objective in a common direction. (6) SUBORDINATION OF INDIVIDUAL INTERESTS TO THE GENERAL INTERESTS : The interests of one person should not take priority over the interests of the organization as a whole. (7) REMUNERATION : Many variables, such as cost of living, supply of qualified personnel, general business conditions, and success of the business, should be considered in determining a worker's rate of pay. (8) CENTRALIZATION : Fayol defined centralization as lowering the importance of the subordinate role. Decentralization is increasing the importance. The degree to which centralization or decentralization should be adopted depends on the specific organization in which the manager is working. (9) SCALAR CHAIN : Managers in hierarchies are part of a chain like authority scale. Each manager, from the first line supervisor to the president, possess certain amounts of authority. The President possesses the most authority; the first line supervisor the least. Lower level managers should always keep upper level managers informed of their work activities. (10) ORDER : For the sake of efficiency and coordination, all materials and people related to a specific kind of work should be treated as equally as possible. (11) EQUITY : All employees should be treated as equally as possible. (12) STABILITY OF TENURE OF PERSONNEL : Retaining productive employees should always be a high priority of management. Recruitment and Selection Costs, as well as increased product-reject rates are usually associated with hiring new workers. (13) INITIATIVE : Management should take steps to encourage worker initiative, which is defined as new or additional work activity undertaken through self direction. (14) ESPIRIT DE CORPS : Management should encourage harmony and general good feelings among employees.

Que : Explain Levels of Management.

In many small business enterprises, the owner is the only member of the management team. But as the size of an organization increases, a more sophisticated organizational structure is required. Every organization or company has a particular hierarchy. There are different levels in an organization. Basically there are three levels :

(1) Top Level Management
(2) Middle Level Management
(3) First / Supervisory Level Management

(1) Top Level Management : Top Level Management comprises board of directors, chief executives or managing directors. CEO, President, Vice President, Chairman fall into the category of Top Level Management. The top management is the ultimate authority. They will decide goals and policies for an enterprise. They focus on planning and coordinating functions. Overall activities of company depend on top level management. They are also responsible towards the shareholders for the performance of the enterprise. Top Level Managers are responsible for taking major decisions for the organization. Functions of top level management are as below :

- Develops and reviews long-range plans and strategies
- Evaluates overall performance
- Involved in selection of key personnel
- Consult subordinate managers for problems

(2) Middle Level Management : Middle Level Management is a link between Top Level and First Level Management. Middle level incorporates branch managers and departmental managers. They are accountable for the functioning of their department. They will do organization and directional function. There are chances for promotion for this level and goes to top level. Middle level managers execute the plans of the organization accordance with the goals and policies of the top management. Middle level management is a training opportunity for the higher positions. Functions of Middle Level Management are as below :

- Makes plans of intermediate range
- Analyze managerial performance to determine capability
- Establishes departmental policies
- Reviews daily and weekly reports on production or sales.
- Prepare long-range plans for review by top management

(3) First Level Management : It is also known as supervisory / operative level of management. It consist of supervisor, foreman, section officer, superintendent, workers and jobbers. People working in lower level management are responsible for direction and controlling functions of management. They are responsible for the quality as well as quantity of production. Lower level managers are mediators between workers and higher level management. This level is sometimes sub divided into two levels: a job level consisting of jobbers who are in charge of gang of workers, which is the lowest level and supervisory level of foreman and supervisors who are at upper lower level. Lower level management represents actually operating level management.

From the view point of function of management, planning is least at this level. The supervisors take part in planning of his department. Their main task is to implement the plans prepared by the top management. There is more staffing or personnel management at this level. The lower level is wide-ranging. The directing function is most important at this level, because it has direct control over employees who are actually engaged in production.

Here are the functions of first level management :

- Makes detailed, short-range operational plans
- Reviews performance of subordinates
- Supervises day-to-day operations.
- Make specific task assignments
- Maintains close contact with employees involved in operations.

Conclusion :

The policies and goals of the company are to be place before the workers. A supervisor is a link between the management and workers. He has to represent to top management the problems of workers.

The functions related to production are equally important at the lower level of management. The directives of the upper management concerning production are to be carried out at the lower level only. To achieve the targets of production, the lower level has to ensure that schedule of production fixed, production process is continued uninterruptedly and quality in controlled.

Que : List 14 points guideline for manager of Deming.	Que : "Management is a Science as well as an Art" - Explain
W. Edwards Deming proposed 14 points as a guideline for top managers. Following are the points suggested by Deming :	**Management as Process :** George R. Terry is of the opinion that management is a distinct process consisting of planning, organizing, directing and controlling, which are performed to determine and accomplish objectives by the use of people and resources. Management is a process in the sense that it is concerned with planning, executing and controlling the activities of an enterprise. It is basically concerned with the interrelationship of people at work, mainly with directing the performance rather than with quantum of work done.

W. Edwards Deming proposed 14 points as a guideline for top managers. Following are the points suggested by Deming :

1. "*Create constancy of purpose towards improvement*". Replace short-term reaction with long-term planning.

2. "*Adopt the new philosophy*". The implication is that management should actually adopt his philosophy, rather than merely expect the workforce to do so.

3. "*Cease dependence on inspection*". If variation is reduced, there is no need to inspect manufactured items for defects, because there won't be any.

4. "*Move towards a single supplier for any one item*." Multiple suppliers mean variation between feedstocks.

5. "*Improve constantly and forever*". Constantly strive to reduce variation.

6. "*Institute training on the job*". If people are inadequately trained, they will not all work the same way, and this will introduce variation.

7. "*Institute leadership*". Deming makes a distinction between leadership and mere supervision. The latter is quota- and target-based.

8. "*Drive out fear*". Deming sees management by fear as counter- productive in the long term, because it prevents workers from acting in the organization's best interests.

9. "Break down barriers between departments".

10. "*Eliminate slogans*". Another central TQM idea is that it's not people who make most mistakes - it's the process they are working within.

11. "*Eliminate management by objectives*". Deming saw production targets as encouraging the delivery of poor-quality goods.

12. "*Remove barriers to pride of workmanship*". Many of the other problems outlined reduce worker satisfaction.

13. "*Institute education and self-improvement*".

14. "*The transformation is everyone's job*".

Management as Process : George R. Terry is of the opinion that management is a distinct process consisting of planning, organizing, directing and controlling, which are performed to determine and accomplish objectives by the use of people and resources. Management is a process in the sense that it is concerned with planning, executing and controlling the activities of an enterprise. It is basically concerned with the interrelationship of people at work, mainly with directing the performance rather than with quantum of work done.

Management as Art :

- **Personal Skills and Knowledge** : Art is practical implementation of personal skills and knowledge to achieve outcome. Just like an Artist, a manager applies his knowledge and skills to coordinate the efforts of the people.

- **Personalized Process :** Art is a personalized process and every artist or a human being has his own style. Management is also a personalized process. Every manager has his own perception about the problem and accordingly he decides the solution for problem.

- **Creativity** : Art is essentially creative and the success of an artist is measured by the result he achieves. Management is creative like any other art. In case any new situations arise, it converts available resources into output and works towards the goal achievement earn.

- **Practical Experience :** As we know art is practice based. For perfection, it has to be practiced continuously e.g. Music, Dancing, and Painting are also arts. Management needs sufficiently long period of experience in managing.

Management as Science : Science refers to a systematic body of knowledge acquired through observation, experimentation and intelligent speculation. Management deals with the systematic knowledge of acquiring the skill of getting things done through others. Management is an accepted science as a way of solving problems and taking decisions. A scientific attitude is absolutely essential for a manager in problem solving and decision making. Management is neither a science nor an art but is combination of both.

Que : Explain Closed and Open System View of Organization.	Que : Explain Formal and Informal Organization.

<u>Closed System View of Organizations</u> : According to Louis E. Boone and David L Kurtz, "Closed system are sets of interacting elements operating without any exchange with the environment in which they exist. This definition implies that closed system require no inputs – human , financial etc. – from the external environment in which they exist. But no organization can be totally closed system. For example, a closed system like a wind up alarm clock requires outside intervention when it slows down or goes out of order. Thus a totally closed system is only a theoretical concept.
 	
The two basic characteristics of a closed system are :
   (1) It is perfectly deterministic and predictable
   (2) There is no exchange between the system and the external environment.
 	
If one college campus converts into deemed university, then it becomes closed system. To some extent, you can predict styles of exam, schemes, and syllabus as there is no exchange with any affiliated university. So rules and norms somehow remain predictable.
 	
<u>Open System View of Organizations</u> : Traditional closed system views ignored the influence of the external environment. This sometimes led to the failure of plans and inefficient handling of resources. Boone and Kurtz define an open system as "A set of elements that interact with each other and the environment, and whose structure originates as a result of interaction."
 	
The open system concept is based on the assumption that no system is totally deterministic or predictable because of the uncertainties in the external environment.
 	
For example, If one college is affiliated with some university, then it is an open system because there is exchange with external environment. You cannot predicts rules and norms for upcoming semester as university can change rules. Thus, system remains unpredictable because of uncertainties in external environment.
 	
Tihar jail is a closed system while an advertising agency is an example of open system.
 	
An Organization is a system consisting of several subsystem which interact with another. The Organization is a subsystem of a larger system.
	A Formal Organization is a group of people working together cooperatively under authority. This Organization depends on authority, responsibility and accountability.
	
	An informal organization is "a network of personal and social relation not established or required by the formal organization.
	
	An informal organization focuses on people and their relationships whereas a formal organization focuses on official positions in terms of authority, responsibility and accountability.
	
	In an informal organization, 'power' is associated with a person but in a formal organization, 'power' is associated with a position. In other words, in informal organizations, power is purely personal in origin, while in formal organizations , power is institutional in origin. The informal organization may or may not support the goals and objectives established by the formal organizations.
	
	Informal relationships develop spontaneously, supplementing or modifying the formal relationship established by the management. For example, an informal relationship may be established among people who may have lunch together. Informal relationship can help a company attain organizational goals as people may find it easier to seek help from someone they know informally.
	
	The emergence of informal organizations within a formal framework is a natural process. Informal groups are formed to share their common attitudes, beliefs etc.
	
	<u>Formal Organization</u> :
	
	  • Official
	  • Authority and Responsibility
	  • Position
	  • Delegated by Management
	  • Rules
	  • Reward and Penalties
	
	<u>Informal Organization</u> :
	
	  • Unofficial
	  • Power and Politics
	  • Person
	  • Given by group
	  • Norms
	  • Sanctions

Que : Explain Characteristics / Features of Management.

(1) <u>Management is Goal Oriented</u> : Management is highly goal oriented activity. The success of management can be measured in terms of the achievement of predetermined goals or objectives of an organization.

(2) <u>Management is Continuous</u> : Management involves continuous handling of problems and issues. It is an ongoing process. It includes the problem identification and finding out the solution by taking appropriate steps.

(3) <u>Management is Time Oriented</u> : Management is nothing but a race against time. In today's world everyone wants to impress customers. Customer is most impressed if he receives service in time. Management ensures that the production schedules are met and the targets are achieved.

(4) <u>Management is a Group Activity</u> : Management is more concerned with the group activity rather than individual's performance. The efforts measured are in terms of groups to achieve predetermined goals or objectives.

(5) <u>Management integrates Human, Physical and Financial Resources</u> : In any organization, the different resources used are humans, machines, materials, financial assets, building etc. Humans have to work with non-human resources to perform their jobs. The management plays very important role here. It integrates human efforts to those non-human resources. It brings harmony among available resources.

Management is concerned with guidelines to the human as well as the resources of the organization to achieve the organizational goal. Management is linked with other fields of study Anthropology, Economics, Philosophy and Political Science.

Management is basically a human process which deals with interpersonal relationship in any organization in the form of formal relationships of superior subordinates and peers. Management basically deals with the living human resources compared to the other non-human resources like machines, material, money etc. Management is a specialty in dealing with matters of time and human relationship.

Que : <u>"Management is a specialty in dealing with matters of time and human relationship." – Justify</u> (Same Answer)

Que : Innovative Management for Turbulent Times

We are living in turbulent times. Turbulent times is a climate in which there is no stability for the business entities and there is change for all angles you never know what to expect. We have now entered the period of problem which contains climate change, financial instability, high unemployment and the financial consequences of an aging society.

There are problems of recession. Technology is changing continuously and businesses don't know how it will affect them. The million dollar question is how one is supposed to manager his business in such turbulent times. The second question that comes to one's mind is what happen to innovation. Innovations are rising like anything. But companies have faced this challenge and have planned to fight with this problem. Many thinkers believes that the innovation process should not stop but more innovation does not necessary mean smart innovation. These innovations should also responsible for the revival of business. Smart innovation is built on effective competence for renewal and superior management capabilities. Innovation gives growth and competitive advantaged to the company. The major challenge for the management is to reduce the risk element and the chances of failure in the innovation. The method to achieving this result is incremental innovation with cumulative impact.

Que : <u>Explain Management as Profession.</u>

A field or a concept is characterized as profession when the following special features are incorporated :

1. Systematic body of knowledge of a profession
2. Importance of its learning and proper organization of the science
3. Entry restricted on the basis of examination or education or training
4. Dominance of service motive

Management qualifies all test of a profession. It is backed by a systematic body of knowledge. A number of management principles have been developed which need proper learning and education. Management is more creative rather than adaptive. It also deals with ethical and social responsibilities towards the society.

Another important development in the field of management has been that the professional management consultants are growing both in number and quality. Professional attributes are very much present in the concept of management.

Unit - 2 : Management History

Que – Explain the principles and techniques of Scientific Management Approach. (Taylor)

Scientific Management is often called Taylorism. Its main objective was improving economic efficiency. It was one of the earliest attempts to apply science to management. The core ideas of scientific management were developed by Frederick Winslow Taylor in the 1880s and 1890s, and were first published in his book Shop Management and The Principles of Scientific Management. While working as a lathe operator and foreman at Midvale Steel, Taylor noticed the natural differences in productivity between workers.

Soldering and Faulty Wage System : Taylor observed that some workers were more talented than others but they are unmotivated . He observed that most workers who are forced to perform repetitive tasks work at slowest rate. Workers deliberately work at slowest rate because they will not get benefit if they give more output. Workers feared that if they gave more output , others would lose their job. He therefore proposed that the work practice that had been developed in most work environments was crafted, intentionally or unintentionally, to be very inefficient in its execution. Faulty Wage System is responsible for this problem. The Problem is often called "Soldering." Soldering means deliberately work at slow rate

Rest Break : Taylor suggested that labor should include rest breaks so that workers can recover themselves from mental or physical fatigue.

Time and Motion Study : Taylor observed that every work includes some necessary and unnecessary movements. Unnecessary movements take away some time and energy from workers. If these movements were avoided, the performance and the output would increase.
The main steps are
(1) Observing the motion of the workers while working
(2) Identify necessary and unnecessary movements,
(3) With a stop watch count time of unnecessary movements
(4) Eliminate unnecessary movements,
(5) Develop the movements that are necessary and standard.

Pig Iron Experiment : Taylor is best known for his pig iron experiments Workers loaded pigs of iron onto rail cars. Their daily average output was 12.5. Taylor believed that output could be 48 tons by applying Scientific Management approach. After scientifically applying different combination of procedure, techniques and tools, Taylor succeeded in getting that level of productivity.

Differential Payment / Piece-rate incentive system :
Taylor proposed the setting up of differential piece rate system of payment.
(1) Fix the standard level of production
(2) Workers producing less than the standard receive less payment.
(3) Workers producing more than the standard receive higher payment

Differential Piece Rate Payment motivates the workers to perform better than the standards set. Taylor proposed that there is one best method to do any Job. He believed that decisions based upon tradition and rules of thumb should be replaced by precise procedure developed after careful study of an individual at work.

Criticism of Scientific Management :

(1) Taylor is only concerned with output / productivity. Taylor has totally overlooked other aspects of management like finance, accounting, marketing etc.
(2) Union leaders felt that it was an exploitation of the workers.
(3) Human element is absent in this theory.
(4) The moral of the worker would go down if he did not complete his target.

Extra Points in Scientific Management Theory :

(1) Scientific Management needs the cooperation of the workers and the management at various stages.
(2) The workers should understand the point of view of the management in increasing the production and the profitability of the company.
(3) Taylor advocates group harmony by eliminating the dissatisfaction amongst the works.
(4) The movement of material within the company should be scientifically done.
(5) Taylor emphasized the scientific selection of people and the need for appropriate training. He developed the concept of work : "one best way of doing a job"
(6) He gave the concept of functional foremanship. As per this concept, he explained the division of functional authority. The supervisors were delegated the authorities in their specialized fields.

The theory was extended by Henry Grant, Frank Gilberth and Lillian Gilberth. Henry Grant had defined new payment system and flow chart for work. While Lillian couple had catalogued seventeen different hand motions such as "grasp", "hold" for work.

Que : Explain the contribution of Henry Gantt and Gilbreth to Management History.	Que : Explain Maslow's Hierarchy of Needs.

Henry Gantts's Contribution in Scientific Management :

Henry Gantt was a consulting engineer who specialized in control systems for shop scheduling. Grantt saw the importance of the human element in production and introduced the concept of motivation as used in industry today.

He introduced two new features in Taylor's pay incentive scheme. First, every worker who finished a day's assigned work load was to win a 50 cent bonus for that day. Second even the foreman was rewarded with a bonus for each worker who reached the daily standard, plus an extra bonus if all the workers reached it. Gantt felt that this would motivate a foreman to teach his worker to do 'he job well. Gantt also developed the idea of rating an employee publicly.

Gantt developed the Gantt Charts that provides a graphical representation of the flow of work required to complete a give task. The chart represent each Planned stage of the work, showing both scheduled times and actual time. This chart is precursor of modern day control techniques like Critical Path Techniques (CPM) and Programme Evaluation and Review Technique (PERT)

Frank Gilbreth and Lillian Gilbreth's contribution to Scientific Management Theory :

Frank and Lillian Gilbreth made their contribution to the scientific management movement as a husband –wife team. The Gilbreths turned motion study into an exact science. They used motion pictures for studying and streamlining work motions. They catalogued seventeen different hand motions such as 'grasp', 'hold' thereby paving the way for work simplification. These they called 'therbligs'. Thus, they focused more on the production system along with taking care of the human side of management.

Gilbreths had 12 children. Frank and Lillian Gilbreth were so dedicated to the idea of finding the one best way to do every job that two of their children wrote Cheaper by the Dozen, a humorous recollection of scientific management and motion study applied to Gilbreth household.

The use of the camera in motion study stems from this time and the Gilbreths used micro-motion study in order to record and examine detailed short-cycled movements as well as inventing cyclographs and chronocycle graphs to observe rhythm and movement.

Maslow's hierarchy of needs is a theory in psychology, proposed by Abraham Maslow in his 1943 paper "A Theory of Human Motivation." In 1943, Abraham H. Maslow theorized that people were motivated by a hierarchy of needs. These needs are :

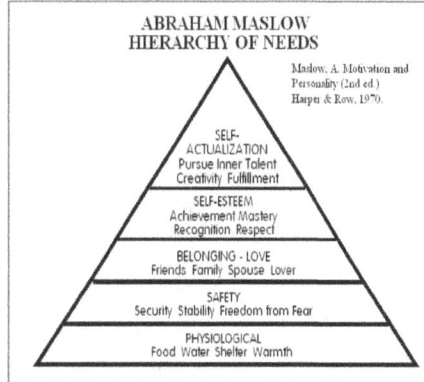

ABRAHAM MASLOW
HIERARCHY OF NEEDS

Maslow, A. Motivation and Personality (2nd ed.) Harper & Row, 1970.

SELF-ACTUALIZATION
Pursue Inner Talent Creativity Fulfillment

SELF-ESTEEM
Achievement Mastery Recognition Respect

BELONGING - LOVE
Friends Family Spouse Lover

SAFETY
Security Stability Freedom from Fear

PHYSIOLOGICAL
Food Water Shelter Warmth

(1) Physiological Needs : These needs are related to the survival and maintenance of life. These include food, clothing, shelter etc.
For the most part, physiological needs are obvious – they are the literal requirements for human survival. If these requirements are not met, the human body simply cannot continue to function.

(2) Safety Needs : These consist of safety against murder, fire, accident, security against unemployment etc.

(3) Social Needs : These needs include need for love , affection, belonging or association with family, friends and other social groups.
After physiological and safety needs are fulfilled, the third layer of human needs are interpersonal and involve feelings of belongingness. The need is especially strong in childhood

(4) Ego or esteem needs : These are needs derived from recognition, status , achievement, power , prestige etc.
Esteem presents the normal human desire to be accepted and valued by others.

(5) Self-fulfillment : It is need to fulfill what a person considers to be his real mission of life
"What a man can be, he must be." This forms the basis of the perceived need for self-actualization. This level of need pertains to what a person's full potential is and realizing that potential.

Que : Discuss the behavioral approach to management. Discuss the Hawthorne experiments in detail.

Scientific Management Approach was concerned with physical mechanical aspects of work. Human element is absent in it. Behavioral approach to management is concerned with human element and human behavior. The behavioral management theory is often called the human relations movement because it addresses the human dimension of work. They believed that a better understanding of human behavior at work such as motivation, conflict, and expectation will improve productivity.

A theory of motivation had three assumptions :
1. Human needs are never completely satisfied
2. Human behavior is motivated by the need for satisfaction
3. Need can be classified according to a hierarchical structure of important

In 1927, a group of researchers led by Elton Mayo and Fritz Roethlisberger of the Harvard Business School were invited to join in the studies at the Hawthorne Works of Western Electric Company, Chicago. The experiment lasted up to 1932. The Hawthorne Experiments brought out that the productivity of the employees is not the function of only physical conditions of work and money wages paid to them. Productivity of employees depends heavily upon the satisfaction of the employees in their work situation.

The Hawthorne experiment consists of four parts.
1.   Illumination Experiment.
2.   Relay Assembly Test Room Experiment.
3.   Interviewing Programme.
4.   Bank Wiring Test Room Experiment.

(1) Illumination Experiment : This experiment was conducted to establish relationship between output and illumination. When the intensity of light was increased, the output also increased. The output showed an upward trend even when the illumination was gradually brought down to the normal level. Therefore, it was concluded that there is no consistent relationship between output of workers and illumination in the factory. There must be some other factor which affected productivity.

(2) Relay Assembly Test Room Experiment :
This phase aimed at knowing not only the impact of illumination on production but also other factors like length of the working day, rest hours, and other physical conditions. In this experiment, a small homogeneous work-group of six girls was constituted. These girls were friendly to each other and were asked to work in a very informal atmosphere under the supervision of a researcher. Productivity and morale increased considerably during the period of the experiment. Productivity went on increasing and stabilized at a high level even when all the improvements were taken away and the pre-test conditions were reintroduced. The researchers concluded that socio-psychological factors such as feeling of being important, recognition, attention, participation, cohesive work-group, and non-directive supervision held the key for higher productivity.

(3) Mass Interview Program : Around 20000 workers have been interviewed. The researchers observed that the replies of the workmen were guarded. Therefore, this approach was replaced by an indirect technique, where the interviewer simply listened to what the workmen had to say. Researcher found that individual performance is motivated by group. Upward communication is important as workers felt that their voices have been heard by authority.

(4) Bank Wiring Test Room Experiment : The experiment was conducted to study a group of workers under conditions which were as close as possible to normal. This group comprised of 14 workers. After the experiment, the production records of this group were compared with their earlier production records. It was observed that the group evolved its own production norms for each individual worker, which was made lower than those set by the management. There are Informal Groups in Organization. Informal Groups sets their own standards which is not compatible with company's standard. Because of this, workers would produce only that much, thereby defeating the incentive system. Those workers who tried to produce more than the group norms were isolated, harassed or punished by the group.

Conclusion : Behavioral science is concerned with the social and psychological aspects of human behavior in organization. Behavioral Approach proves that people working in an organization have their needs and goals, which may differ from the organization's needs and goals. It also proves that individual behavior is closely linked with the behavior of the group to which he belongs. Informal leadership, rather than the formal authority of supervision is more important for group performance. Behavioral Approach considered the human variables within the organization only and the other variables which also played a major role in the functioning of the organization were ignored. In Behavioral approach, concentration was on the lower level of organization and not the middle and the upper level of the organization.

Que : Discuss Systems Approach of Management.

System Approach is the most acceptable approach in the modern management. The major contributories are Herbert A. Simon. George Homons, Philip Selznick etc. This approach considers organization as a unified, directed system of integrated parts. It emphasized that every organization is composed of different parts and one part affect all other parts in a varying degree.

The key concept of system approach is the holistic approach to a problem which indicates that no part or segment of the system can be analyzed accurately without considering the whole system and similarly no system can be conceived without understanding each of the parts of the system.

Following aspects of the system approach should be understood clearly :

(1) System : The term system is derived from Greek Word "synistanai," which means to bring together or combine A System is a set of interdependent parts which together form a unitary whole. The organization is a sub system of four interdependent parts task, structure, people and technology.

(2) Sub-system : Each part of the system as a whole is known as a sub-system. The entire system is integrated with such a characteristic of sub-system in a linear manner. For example, machine shop is a sub-system of production department.

(3) Synergy : Synergy means that the whole (system) is greater than the sum of its parts. Synergy indicates two plus two is greater than four. This implies that departments within an organization which interact cooperative are more productive than they would be if they operated in isolation.

(4) Entropy : Entropy is the tendency of system to run down or die if it does not receive fresh inputs from its environment

(5) Open and Close System : Open system interacts with external environment while close system do not interact with external environment.

(6) System Boundary : Each system has its own boundary which separate it from other system in environment. The boundary is rigid in the close system and is flexible under open system. For example, chemical factory must consider the pollution control as it will affect the surrounding climate

(7) Flow : Input are translated into outputs through the flows. Such flows could be informational or physical. Information, Material and Energy enters into system as input then they undergo into process and results into output. Input comes from outer world and resulted output once again goes to outer world.

(8) Feedback : Feedback is a key process in controlling the system. This is the mechanism of control. Under the feedback process, the results are feedback to original inputs or other parts of the system. Information can be fed back either during the transformation process or at the output stage

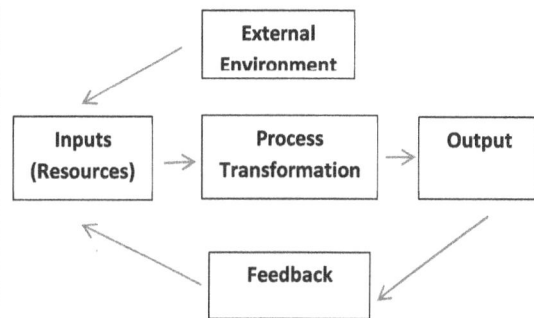

A few years ago, product developers at Motorola Crop. Thought about building a stylish new mobile phone called the Razr. The developers consulted immediately with manufacturing, engineering , purchasing and dealers to discuss feasibility of their idea. Working together, the units of the organization produced a highly successful product in a tight competitive market.

Limitations/ Criticisms :   This approach is theoretical and abstract and is not amenable practice in reality. People have their individual goals. Organization goals and individual goals make the whole system confusing. The system approach is more suitable for a large complex organization, not for small units. The system approach does not contribute to any newer knowledge.

Conclusion : System approach to management advocates that manager should not accept limited view of responsibility. They should not consider their units / departments as an individual and isolated units. Subordinate, Manager and individual department should try to maximize their performance and contribution to all departments of organization.

Que – What is the major task of the manager according to the contingency approach ?

The Contingency approach emerged out of the system approach. It is extension rather a refinement of the system approach. This is also known as the situational theory. According to this theory, there is no best way to manage all situations. In other words, there is no one best way to manage. The contingency approach was developed by managers, consultant and researchers. Paul Hersey and Ken Blanchard developed the contingency of leadership. The contingency approach to management emerged from the real life experience of managers who found that no single approach worked consistently in every situation. The basic idea of this approach is that number management technique or theory is appropriate in all situations. The main determinants of a contingency are related to the external and internal environment of an organization.

Contingency approach advocates that managerial actions and organizational design must be appropriate to the given situation and a particular action is valid only under certain conditions. There is no one best approach to management and it all depends on the situation. In other words, managerial action is contingent upon external environment. There is no one best approach for all situations. What a manager does depends upon a given situation and there is an active inter-relationship between the variables in a situation and the managerial action

Under the contingency approach, the task of the manager can be as under :

(1) To get familiarized with all available techniques
(2) To possess the ability to diagnose the situation properly and in an objective manner by studying the prevailing conditions
(3) The ability to decide that which technique will work best in a given situation.

According to Contingency approach, "The task of managers is to identify which technique will, in a particular situation, under particular circumstances, and at a particular time, best contribute to the attainment of management goals.

An Open System Perspective : Open system thinking is the fundamental characteristic. It is necessary to understand how organizational subsystems combine together to interact with the environment.

A Research Orientation : Contingency researcher believe in translating their observation into tools and situational refinements for more effective management. This is based on the assumption that practical research leads to effective management.

A Multivariate Approach : Multivariate analysis is used to determine how several variables interact to produce an outcome.

Features of contingency approach

1. Management is externally situational: the conditions of the situation will determine which techniques and control system should be designed to fit the particular situation.

2. Management is entirely situational.
3. There is no best way of doing anything.
4. One needs to adapt himself to the circumstances.
5. It is kind of "if" "then" approach
6. It is a practically suited.
7. Management policies and procedures should respond to environment.

There are three major elements of the overall conceptual framework for contingency management; the environment, management concepts and techniques and the contingent relationship between them.

Limitations/ Criticisms of Contingency Approach

(1) This approach suggests that "managerial act depends on situation" but it has not developed the techniques of identifying a particular situation and the appropriateness of a particular techniques to a given situation.

(2) A particular management problem in a given situation might have tacked in a unique manner. But it is very difficult to conclude that it was the best solution in the given situation.

(3) This approach highlights that manager should study the situation. However it falls to develop the skill of anticipating situations to control.

(4) Critics of the contingency approach have blamed it to lack theoretical foundation and are basically intuitive.

(5) Managers need to analyze a situation and use ideas from the various schools of thought to find solution. This is very complex and confusing process.

Que – What are the different approaches to management ? Explain them taking the essence of each approach.

ANSWER OF THIS QUESTION CAN BE GIVEN BY WRITING MAIN POINTS FROM SCIENTIFIC, BEHAVIORAL, SYSTEM AND CONTINGENCY APPROACH. THIS IS SAMPLE ANSWER. NO NEED TO READ IT AS YOU CAN WRITE DOWN FROM PREVIOUS QUESTIONS.

Scientific Management Approach

Scientific Management is often called Taylorism. Its main objective was improving economic efficiency. It was one of the earliest attempts to apply science to management. The core ideas of scientific management were developed by Frederick Winslow Taylor in the 1880s and 1890s, and were first published in his book Shop Management and The Principles of Scientific Management. While working as a lathe operator and foreman at Midvale Steel, Taylor noticed the natural differences in productivity between workers. Taylor observed that every work includes some necessary and unnecessary movements. Unnecessary movements take away some time and energy from workers. If these movements were avoided, the performance and the output would increase. Differential Piece Rate Payment motivates the workers to perform better than the standards set. Taylor proposed that there is one best method to do any Job. The movement of material within the company should be scientifically done. Taylor emphasized the scientific selection of people and the need for appropriate training. He developed the concept of work : "one best way of doing a job"

Behavioral Approach to Management

Scientific Management Approach was concerned with physical mechanical aspects of work. Human element is absent in it. Behavioral approach to management is concerned with human element and human behavior. The behavioral management theory is often called the human relations movement because it addresses the human dimension of work. They believed that a better understanding of human behavior at work such as motivation, conflict, and expectation will improve productivity. Behavioral science is concerned with the social and psychological aspects of human behavior in organization. Behavioral Approach proves that people working in an organization have their needs and goals, which may differ from the organization's needs and goals. It also proves that individual behavior is closely linked with the behavior of the group to which he belongs. Informal leadership, rather than the formal authority of supervision is more important for group performance.

System Approach to Management

System Approach is the most acceptable approach in the modern management. The major contributories are Herbert A. Simon. George Homons, Philip Selznick etc. This approach considers organization as a unified, directed system of integrated parts. It emphasized that every organization is composed of different parts and one part affect all other parts in a varying degree. System approach to management advocates that manager should not accept limited view of responsibility. They should not consider their units / departments as an individual and isolated units. Subordinate, Manager and individual department should try to maximize their performance and contribution to all departments of organization.

Contingency Approach to Management

According to this theory, there is no best way to manage all situations. In other words, there is no one best way to manage. The contingency approach was developed by managers, consultant and researchers. Paul Hersey and Ken Blanchard developed the contingency of leadership. The contingency approach to management emerged from the real life experience of managers who found that no single approach worked consistently in every situation.

Universal Approach to Management

This approach considered management as a process. The process of management consists of several functions like planning, organizing, directing, controlling. The pioneering work was done by Henry Fayol. According to this approach, authority originates at top and flows downwards in unbroken manner,

Quantitative Approach

This approach primarily focuses on the use of mathematical models. This approach strived to resolve the problems amenable for quantitative analysis like transportation problems, linear programming etc. It provides an objective base for decision making.

Que : Distinguish Theory X and Theory Y given by Douglas MecGregor.

Social psychologist Douglas McGregor studied the general behavior of human beings and classified such behavior into two parts which is popularly known as Theory X and Theory Y.

Theory X

Theory X revolves around the traditional assumption about the human behavior that they are pessimistic in nature. The basic assumptions of Theory X about worker's behavior are – they dislike the work, they are unwilling to assume responsibility, they are dull and not ambitious, they avoid any assigned work and so should be supervised closely. Douglas McGregor through his research support challenged these assumptions because they are untrue in most of the circumstances.

Theory Y

He propounded an alternative theory y which poses optimistic behavior patterns of the workers. These assumptions highlights that workers are ready to do hard work, they are ready to assume responsibility, they exercise self-imposed disciple avoiding the need of close supervision, they possess the capacity to innovate, they get psychic pleasure in doing the work and consider work as rest or play

Theory X assumes that the average person :

- Dislikes work and attempts to avoid it.
- Has no ambition, wants no responsibility, and would rather follow than lead.
- Is self-centered and therefore does not care about organizational goals.
- Resists change.
- Is gullible and not particularly intelligent.

Theory Y makes the following general assumptions:
- Work can be as natural as play and rest.
- People will be self-directed to meet their work objectives if they are committed to them.
- Most people can handle responsibility because creativity and ingenuity are common in the population.

McGregor argued that the mangers should change their mindset about theory X and should motivate the employees taking into account the set of theory Y assumptions. It will contribute to the better results through tapping the creative and innovative capabilities of the employees

Theory Z by William Ouchi

Willaim Ouchi conducted the research on both American and Japanese management approaches to identify the underlying critical factors for success. These research findings resulted into the evolution of new theory known as "Theory Z." Theory Z combines the positive aspects of both American and Japanese management styles. Theory Z approaches considers the following issues :

Main Points of Theory Z

(1) Job security to employees to ensure their loyalty, committed behavior and long-term association with the company they serve.

(2) It also emphasizes the job rotation for the development of the cross-sectional skills.

(3) It advocates the participation of employees in the decision –making process.

(4) The organization is concerned about the development of employees through providing training opportunities and also in the well-being of the employees and their families.

Theory Z is an approach to management based upon a combination of American and Japanese management philosophies and characterized by, among other things, long-term job security, consensual decision making, slow evaluation and promotion procedures, and individual responsibility within a group context.

Research shows that, since the boom years of Japanese industry in the 1980's and 90's, the effect of Ouichi's theory Z has been fairly mixed. Some suggest that its impact has been limited. Others suggest that organizations that adopt Theory Z-type practices reap big rewards in terms of employee satisfaction, motivation and performance. Either way, there is no doubt that William Ouichi left his mark on the development of management thinking.

Que : Explain Quantitative Approach to Management. (Out of Syllabus)

During World War II, mathematicians, physicists, and other scientists joined together to solve military problems. The quantitative school of management is a result of the research conducted during World War II. The quantitative approach to management involves the use of quantitative techniques, such as statistics, information models, and computer simulations, to improve decision making. This school consists of several branches, described in the following sections.

Management Science

The management science school emerged to treat the problems associated with global warfare. Today, this view encourages managers to use mathematics, statistics, and other quantitative techniques to make management decisions. Managers can use computer models to figure out the best way to do something — saving both money and time. Managers use several science applications. Mathematical forecasting helps make projections that are useful in the planning process.

Inventory modeling helps control inventories by mathematically establishing how and when to order a product. Queuing theory helps allocate service personnel or workstations to minimize customer waiting and service cost.

Operations management

Operations management is a narrow branch of the quantitative approach to management. It focuses on managing the process of transforming materials, labor, and capital into useful goods and/or services. The product outputs can be either goods or services; effective operations management is a concern for both manufacturing and service organizations. Operations management today pays close attention to the demands of quality, customer service, and competition.

Management information systems

Management information systems (MIS) is the most recent subfield of the quantitative school. A management information system organizes past, present, and projected data from both internal and external sources and processes it into usable information, which it then makes available to managers at all organizational levels. The information systems are also able to organize data into usable and accessible formats. As a result, managers can identify alternatives quickly, evaluate alternatives by using a spreadsheet program, pose a series of "what-if" questions, and finally, select the best alternatives based on the answers to these questions.

Que : Explain Classical / Universal Approach to Management. (Out of Syllabus)

This approach considered management as a process. The process of management consists of several functions like planning, organizing, directing and controlling. The pioneering work was done by Henry Fayol. The process concept was universally accepted and became the base around which the modern theory of management developed. Some other contributories of this approach are Max. Weber, Marry Parker, Follett Chester 1 Barnard, Colonel L. Urwick, James Mooney, Railey etc.

Main points of this Classical /Universal approach

(1) Management is a process consisting of several elements like planning, organizing, directing and controlling.
(2) The authority originates at top and flows downwards in an unbroken manner passing through scalar chain.
(3) The authority and responsibility should be equated and be communication in writing.
(4) The span of control should be limited depending upon nature of work. In repetitive work, the span can be longer but for non-repetitive work, it should be shorter.
(5) Authorities can be delegated but responsibilities are absolute and cannot be delegated.
(6) This approach emphasized the important human resources as compared to non-human resources like machine and material.
(7) Max Webber's concept of bureaucracy emphasized the rational division of activities to be integrated into a formal hierarchical structure.

Limitations / Criticisms

(1) This approach emphasized the mechanistic organization structure which ignored the psychological and social need of people like social acceptance, esteem and self-actualization. Some principles developed under this approach are contradictory e.g. the principles of unity of command of superior and the principles of specialization of subordinates do not stand simultaneously.

If any questions related to Henry Fayol, Classical Theory, Administration Theory, Modern Theory will be asked, then you need to merge this answer with "Principles of Management" (Unit-1)

Que : Explain Schools (thoughts) of Management.

The schools of management thought are theoretical frameworks for the study of management. Each of the schools of management thought are based on somewhat different assumptions about human beings and the organizations for which they work.

Disagreement exists as to the exact number of management schools. Different writers have identified as few as three and as many as twelve. Those discussed below include (1) the classical school, (2) the behavioral school, (3) the quantitative or management science school, (4) the systems school, (5) and the contingency school.

THE CLASSICAL SCHOOL

The classical school is the oldest formal school of management thought. Its roots pre-date the twentieth century. The classical school of thought generally concerns ways to manage work and organizations more efficiently. Three areas of study that can be grouped under the classical school are scientific management, administrative management, and bureaucratic management.

(1) SCIENTIFIC MANAGEMENT.
Scientific management was introduced in an attempt to create a mental revolution in the workplace. It can be defined as the systematic study of work methods in order to improve efficiency. Frederick W. Taylor was its main proponent. Other major contributors were Frank Gilbreth, Lillian Gilbreth, and Henry Gantt.

(2) ADMINISTRATIVE MANAGEMENT.
Administrative management focuses on the management process and principles of management. Henri Fayol is the major contributor to this school of management thought.
Fayol argued that management was a universal process consisting of functions, which he termed planning, organizing, commanding, coordinating, and controlling. Fayol believed that all managers performed these functions and that the functions distinguished management as a separate discipline of study apart from accounting, finance, and production. Fayol also presented fourteen principles of management.

(3) BUREAUCRATIC MANAGEMENT
Bureaucratic management focuses on the ideal form of organization. Max Weber was the major contributor to bureaucratic management. Based on observation, Weber concluded that many early organizations were inefficiently managed, with decisions based on personal relationships and loyalty. He proposed that a form of organization, called a bureaucracy, characterized by division of labor, hierarchy, formalized rules, impersonality, and the selection and promotion of employees based on ability, would lead to more efficient management. Weber also contended that managers' authority in an organization should be based not on tradition or charisma but on the position held by managers in the organizational hierarchy.

THE BEHAVIORAL SCHOOL

The behavioral school of management thought developed, in part, because of perceived weaknesses in the assumptions of the classical school. The classical school emphasized efficiency, process, and principles. Some felt that this emphasis disregarded important aspects of organizational life, particularly as it related to human behavior. Thus, the behavioral school focused on trying to understand the factors that affect human behavior at work. It includes :
(1) Human Relations (Hawthorne Experiments)
(2) Behavioral Science

THE QUANTITATIVE SCHOOL
The quantitative school focuses on improving decision making via the application of quantitative techniques. Its roots can be traced back to scientific management. It includes ;
(1) Management Science
(2) Operations Management
(3) Management Information Systems

SYSTEMS SCHOOL

The systems school focuses on understanding the organization as an open system that transforms inputs into outputs. This school is based on the work of a biologist, Ludwig von Bertalanffy, who believed that a general systems model could be used to unite science. Early contributors to this school included Kenneth Boulding, Richard Johnson, Fremont Kast, and James Rosenzweig.

The systems school began to have a strong impact on management thought in the 1960s as a way of thinking about managing techniques that would allow managers to relate different specialties and parts of the company to one another, as well as to external environmental factors. The systems school focuses on the organization as a whole, its interaction with the environment, and its need to achieve equilibrium.

CONTINGENCY SCHOOL

The contingency school focuses on applying management principles and processes as dictated by the unique characteristics of each situation. It emphasizes that there is no one best way to manage and that it depends on various situational factors, such as the external environment, technology, organizational characteristics, characteristics of the manager, and characteristics of the subordinates

CONTEMPORARY "SCHOOLS" OF MANAGEMENT THOUGHT

Management research and practice continues to evolve and new approaches to the study of management continue to be advanced. This section briefly reviews two contemporary approaches: total quality management (TQM) and the learning organization. While neither of these management approaches offer a complete theory of management, they do offer additional insights into the management field.

Unit - 3 : Organization Structure and Design

Que : Define "Organization." Explain types of organization.

"Organization is a system of co-operative activities of two or more persons." Organization is essentially a matter of relationship of man to man, job to job and department to department. Organization is the process of dividing up of the activities which are necessary to any purpose and arranging them in groups which are assigned to individuals. Organization is necessary for attaining maximum efficiency with minimum of resources.

There are three main types of organization structure.
1) **Line organization**
2) **Functional organization**
3) **Line and Staff organization.**

Line Organization
(Oldest and Simplest Style)

In this type of organization, the line of authority flows directly from top to bottom and the line of responsibility flows from bottom to top in opposite direction. Each departmental head has complete control over his section and he is fully authorized to select his labor, staff, purchases of raw materials, stores and to set the standards of output etc. The responsibility of each departmental head is clearly defined. Each department works as a self-supporting unit.

Advantages

1. **Simplicity :** It is easy to establish and simple to understand. The entire activities are broadly grouped into departments. Each departmental head having complete command over his department.

2. **Strong in discipline** : Due to unity of command and unified control it is possible to maintain strict discipline. The duties and responsibilities of each individual are clearly defined.

3. **Unity of command** : It establishes clear cut superior subordinate relationships. Each subordinate is responsible to only one superior. This develops a sense of responsibility and loyalty.

Disadvantages

1. **Undue reliance :** Loss of one or two capable men may put the organization in difficulties.

2. **Personal limitations :** In this type of organization an individual executive cannot do justice to all different activities, because cannot be specialized in all trades.

3. **Overload of work :** Departmental heads are overloaded with various routine jobs hence they can not spend time for important managerial functions like planning, development, budgeting etc.

Functional Organization

F.W. Taylor suggested functional organization, because it was difficult to find all-round persons qualified to work at-middle management levels in the line organizations. In this type of organizations specialists like production engineer, design engineer, maintenance engineer, purchase officer etc. are employed.

Each specialist is supposed to give his functional advice to all other foremen and workers. Each specialist is authorized to give orders to workers, but only in regard of his field of specialization.

The main feature of functional organization is the division of work and specialization. In each department, there is one expert. An expert is not only a counselor but also an administrator. He advices his subordinates. An Expert does not only bear responsibility of his department but also bear responsibility of all departments. For example, Purchase Manager will take responsibility of purchasing items for all departments. HR Manager will take responsibility of recruitment of all departments.

Advantages

1. **Separation of work** : In functional organization mental work has been separated from routine work. Specialized and skilled supervisory attention is given to workers. The result is increase in rate of production and improved quality of work.

2. **Ease of selection and training** : Functional organization is based upon expert knowledge. The availability of guidance through experts make is possible to train the workers properly in comparatively sort span of time.

3. It helps in mass production by standardization and specialization.

Disadvantages

1. **Indiscipline** : Since the workers receive instructions from number of specialists it leads to confusion to whom they should follow.

2. **Shifting of Responsibility** : It is difficult fro the top management to locate responsibility for the satisfactory work. Everybody tries to shift responsibilities on others for the faults and failures.

3. **Increase in Cost** : High salary is paid to the experts employed. This increases the total cost of the job.

Line and Staff Organization

The line and staff organization combines the line organization with staff departments that support and advise line department. In each department, there is one expert and some line personnels / line officials. Line official will do all managerial work and expert will give advice to line official or line personnel.

Line and staff organization is that in which the line heads are assisted by specialist staff. The line maintains discipline and stability, staff provides experts information and helps to improve overall efficiency. Thus the staff are thinkers while the line are doers.

Advantages

1. Planned Specialization : The line and staff is a duplex organization, dividing the whole work into creative plan and action plan. The creative plan is concerned with original thinking and the action plan takes care of the execution of work.

2. Availability of specialized knowledge : The staff with expert knowledge provides opportunities to the line officers for adopting rational multidimensional views towards a problem. Therefore it helps to take sound decisions.

3. Adaptability to progressive business. This type of organization contains good features of both line as well as functional organization. Specialized staff can devoted their time for planning, method study research, collection of data etc.,

4. Less wastage & Improved Quality.

Disadvantages

1. Chances of Misinterpretation : Although the expert's advice is available, yet it reaches the workers through line supervisors. The line officers may fail to understand the meaning of advice and there is always a risk of misunderstanding and misinterpretation.

2. Expensive : The overhead cost of the product increases because of high salaried specialized staff.

3. Loss of initiative by line executives : If is they start depending too much on staff may lose their initiative drive and ingenuity.

Line Organization

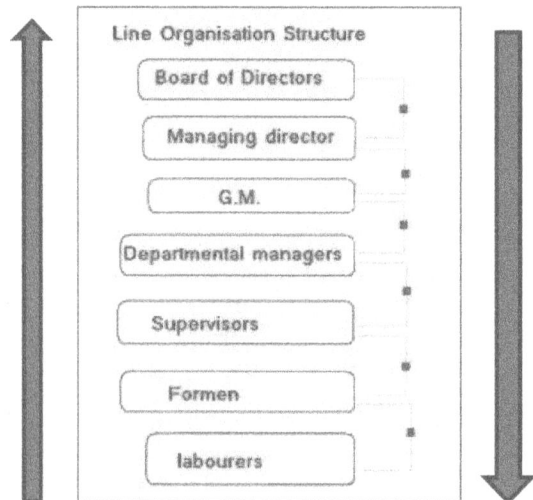

Functional Organization

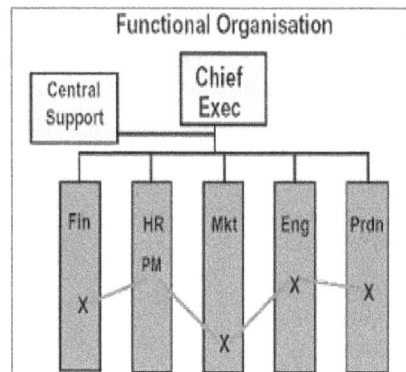

Que – Define 'Departmentalization.' List different types of departmentalization.

Departmentalization is the process of breaking down an enterprise into various departments. How jobs are grouped together is called departmentalization. A Department is an organization unit that is headed by a manager who is responsible for its activities. Departmentation and Division of labour are same things. However technically both are different. Both emphasize on the use of the specialized knowledge, but depratmentation has higher management level strategic considerations while the division of labour has a lower level operating considerations.

Aim : To group activities and personnel to make manageable units.

Types / Methods/Basis of Departmentalization

There are five common forms of departmentalization

(1) Functional Departmentalization
(2) Geographical Departmentalization
(3) Product Departmentalization
(4) Process Departmentalization
(5) Customer Departmentalization

FUNCTIONAL DEPARTMENTALIZATION

It groups jobs according to function.

Functional departmentalization defines departments by the functions each one performs such as accounting or purchasing. Every Organization must perform certain jobs in order to do its work. For example, Manufacturing, Production, R & D, Purchasing etc. Same kinds of jobs are grouped together in departments. This kind of departmentalization includes persons with same knowledge or skills (like Accounting Department having persons of commerce, Marketing Department having MBA persons). As in department people with same skill and knowledge are there. Their focus becomes narrow and they cannot appreciate each other's work in the same department.

Advantages :-
- Efficiencies from putting together similar specialist and people with common skills, knowledge, and orientations.
- In-depth specialization.
- Co-ordination within functional area.

Limitations :-
- Poor communication across functional areas.
- Limited view of organizational goals.

GEOGRAPHICAL DEPARTMENTALIZATION

It groups jobs according to geographic region.

Geographical departmentalization is an arrangement of departments according to geographic area or territory. It divides works well for international business. Geographical Departmentalization is beneficial when Organization are spread over a wide area. Even each part or areas have different requirement or interests. For example, marketing a product in Western Europe may have different requirements than marketing the same product in Southeast Asia. Market area is broken up into sales territories like Northern, Southern, West, East. The Salesman appointed for each territory report to their regional or territorial manager. These manager again reports to the sales manager who is head of the sales department.

Advantages : -
- More effective and efficient handling of specific regional issues that arise.
- Serve needs of unique geographic markets better.

Limitations :-
- Duplication of functions.
- Can feel isolated from other organizational areas.

PRODUCT DEPARTMENTALIZATION

It groups jobs by product line.

Companies may have multiple products. Like Maruti is producing Alto, Zen, Swift. Large companies are often organized according to the product. All common activities required to produce and market a product are grouped together. Major disadvantages are duplication of resources. Each product requires most of the same functional areas such as finance, marketing, production etc. For example, Samsung manufactures Phones, T.V., Tablet etc. For each product, they have same functional department like marketing, production etc. Thus, it is duplication of functions.

Product Departmentalization has become important for large complex organization.

Advantages :-
- Allows specialization in particular products and services.
- Managers can become experts in their industry.
- Closer to customers.

Limitations :-
- Duplication of functions.
- Limited view of organizational goals.
-

PROCESS DEPARTMENTALIZATION

It groups Jobs On The Basis Of Product Or Customer Flow.

Departmentalization is done on the basis of processing. In manufacturing organizations, the location of manufacturing plant or department can be at different location due to cost of raw material and even labour charges. Even departmentalization can be done depending on the types of machines required. The similar types of machines can be kept at one place e.g. all lathes, all drilling machines, all shapers etc. Activities are grouped into separate sections, each kept at one place.

Advantages :-
- More efficient flow of work activities.

Limitations :-
- Can only be used with certain types of products.

CUSTOMER DEPARTMENTALIZATION

It groups Jobs On The Basis of specific And Unique Customers

Customer divisions are divisions set up to service particular types of clients or customers.Some companies or organization divides the different units based on customers or markets. For example, any PC manufacturing company like HP has different divisions like Consumer PC, Commercial PC, and Workstations etc. Nokia previously had three divisions like Consumer Phone, Business Phone & Smart Phone. Recently Nokia had changed their departmentalization from customer to process base. Now there are only two divisions : Hardware and Software base departmentalization. They will also sell their software to other mobile company. Another example is an educational institution offers regular and extension courses to cater to the needs of different students groups.

Advantages :-
- Customers' needs and problems can be met by specialists

Limitations :-
- Duplication of functions.
- Limited view of organizational goals.

This figure is necessary to get good marks

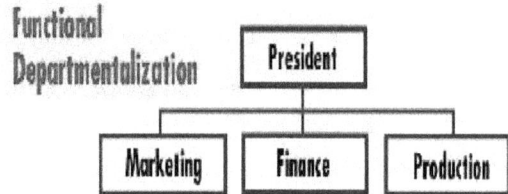

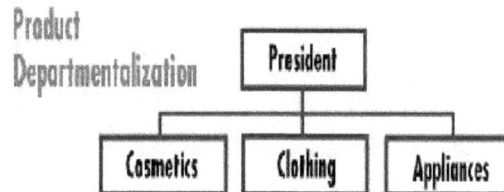

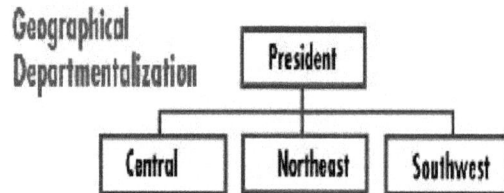

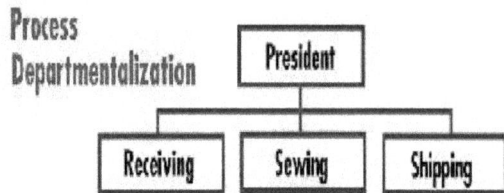

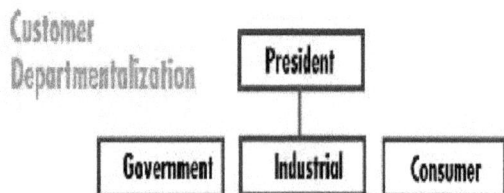

22

Que – Explain centralization and decentralization of authority in detail.

The Process of delegation of authority primarily refers to the centralization or decentralization of authority.

Centralization is the degree to which decision making takes place at upper levels of the organization. If top managers make key decisions with little input from below, then the organization is more centralized. With a centralized structure, line and staff employees have limited authority to carry something out without prior approval. Centralized organizations are known for decreased span of control – a limited number of employees report to a manager, who then report to the next management level.

Decentralization is the degree to which decision making takes place at lower-level employees provide input or actually make decisions, the more decentralization is there. Decentralization seeks to eliminate the unnecessary levels of management and to place authority in the hands of first line managers and staff – thus increasing the span of control with more employees reporting to one manager.

Centralization

(1) Environment is stable.

(2) Lower-level managers are not as capable or experienced at making decisions as upper level managers

(3) Decisions are relatively minor.

(4) Organization is facing a crisis or the risk of company failure.

(5) Company is large.

(6) Lower-level managers do not want a say in decisions.

Decentralization

(1) Environment is complex, uncertain.

(2) Lower-level managers are capable or experienced at making decisions.

(3) Decisions are significant.

(4) Corporate culture is open to allowing managers a say in what happens.

(5) Company is geographically dispersed.

(6) Lower-level managers want a voice in decisions.

Dictatorship is an example of centralized structure and democracy is an example of decentralization.

Advantages of Centralization :

1. Uniformity of decision can be maintained.

2. Quality of decision is better since each and every decision comes from top.

3. Duplication of resource utilization can be prevented.

4. Better integration of planning, directing and control activities.

5. Better coordination of work and efforts of different departments.

6. Flexibility will be high.

Advantages of Decentralization

1. Higher level management can concentrate on work.

2. It develops lower level managers to be promoted to higher level responsibilities.

3. It develops creativity and innovativeness in lower level managers.

4. It increases the morale of the lower level employees.

5. It enables to use the opportunities and local level advantages.

6. It facilitates quick and spot decision making.

7. It helps in locating the responsibilities for wrong decisions.

The degree of centralization and decentralization will depend upon the amount of authority delegated to the lowest level. According to Allen, "Decentralization refers to the systematic effort to delegate to the lowest level of authority except that which can be controlled and exercised at central points. Centralization" is the systematic and consistent reservation of authority at central points in the organization."

Business owners should carefully consider which type of organizational structure to use in their company. Small organizations typically benefit from centralized organizational structures because owners often remain at the forefront of business operations. Larger organizations usually require a more decentralized structure since such companies can have several divisions or departments.

Que : Explain 'Span of Control'. State merits and demerits of a limited span of control. Discuss the factors affecting the span of control.

It states that how many employees can a manager efficiently & effectively manage ? OR *The number of persons who are directly responsible to the executive is called the span of control.*

No single executive should have more people looking to him for controlling & guidance than he can reasonably manage because :-
Limited time
Limited available energy.

The numbers of persons which can be effectively supervised by single executive is 6 to 8 in an average firm. However when activities are routine then executive can supervise 20 to 30.

If span is small, an executive may tend to over supervise & may even do span leading to his subordinates.

If span is large, executive may not be able to supervise his subordinates effectively & they may become careless or feel neglected.

Suppose, you have 4000 workers in Organization. If you divide those workers in 4 groups then you need 1000 Managers. If a span is small, you need 1000 managers and will take large amount of money in terms of Annual Salary of Managers. But Workers will get proper supervision. Now, if we divide those workers in 8 groups then you need 500 Managers. If a span is big then you need 500 managers and will save company's money.

Determinants of Span of Control :

Colonel Urwick stated that the number of subordinates under one superior should range between 4 and 12 depending upon various determinants of the span of control.

(i) Competence of Superior : Competence of Superior is capable enough to handle more subordinates.

(ii) Competence of the subordinates : Competent subordinates disturb less to superior.

(iii) Nature of work : In case of repetitive work, more subordinates can be handled by one superior.

(iv) Means of communication : If subordinates use appropriate media then one superior can handle more number of supervisors.

(v) Leadership Style : In case of autocratic style, the frequency of meeting of subordinates with superior is high.

Merits of Span of Control :

1. Superior can supervise effectively and competently
2. Specialization is encouraged and utilized.
3. Superior can concentrate on limited area of operations.
4. Higher degree of disciplines can be exercised,
5. If results into all the advantages of tall structure.

Demerits of Span of Control :

1. It increases the scalar chain from top to bottom.
2. It demotivates the employees as the contacts between top and bottom is lengthened.
3. It results into all disadvantages of tall structure.

The advantages of a narrow span of control are :

A narrow span of control allows a manager to communicate quickly with the employees under them and control them more easily Feedback of ideas from the workers will be more effective. It requires a higher level of management skill to control a greater number of employees, so there is less management skill required

The advantages of wide span of control are :

There are less layers of management to pass a message through, so the message reaches more employees faster
It costs less money to run a wider span of control because a business does not need to employ as many managers

MOST IMPORTANT

If any question like "key elements / characteristics of Org. Design / Org. Structure / Organization" will be asked, six below mentioned point should be added.

For example :
Describe the six key elements of the organization design ?

The elements are as follows :-
1. Work specialization
2. Departmentalization
3. Chain of command
4. Span of control
5. Centralization and decentralization
6. Formalization.

Then write down little about each point.

Que : What is Organization Structure ? Why are both vertical and horizontal dimensions important to organization structure ?	Que : Discuss about the tall and flat structure of organization.
The Organization structure is a skeleton or a framework that divides the total activities into related groups, develops superior and subordinate relationship among the persons by prescribing the authorities. Thus, it indicates the hierarchy (Persons arranged according to rank), authority structure and reporting relationships. The organizational structure differs from industry to industry. It usually depends upon, 1. **Size of the organization.** 2. **Nature of the product being manufactured.** 3. **Complexity of the problems being faced** **HORIZONTAL DIMENSION** The horizontal dimension defines the basic departmentation i.e. production, marketing etc. Departmentation is the process of diving an enterprise into different parts i.e. smaller, flexible administrative units or sections. **VERTICAL DIMENSION** The Vertical dimension of the structure relate to the creation of hierarchy of superiors and subordinates, leading to the establishment of a managerial structure. It clearly defines that who will report to whom. Considering both horizontal and vertical aspects the formal structure of the organization gets defined. **Importance of Vertical and Horizontal Dimensions** 1. To establish "Superior-Subordinate" relationship 2. To define chain of command 3. To define span of control 4. To establish flow of information 5. To get advantage of specialization 6. To make the role of each individual clear 7. To prevent duplication of work 8. To ensure optimum utilization of resources at minimum possible cost.	**Tall Structure of Organization** **Meaning :** If the span of control is narrow, then there will be many management levels. That is, there will be many managers. This organization structure is called "Tall Organization Structure". **Formal :** In Tall Organisation Structure, a manager has to manage only a few subordinates. Therefore, the relationship between them will be informal. Personal relationships are possible. **Control :** In Tall Organisation Structure, there is a close control because there are few subordinates. **Mistakes :** In Tall Organisation Structure, there are less mistakes because of close supervision and control. **Discipline :** In Tall Organisation Structure, Good discipline can be maintained because there are few subordinates. **Cost :** Tall Organisation Structure is costly because it has many managers **Process :** In Tall Organisation Structure, Decision making and Communication is slow because there are many levels of management. **Flat Structure of Organization** **Meaning :** If the span of control is wide, then there will be fewer management levels. That is, there will be fewer managers. This organization structure is called "Flat Organization Structure". **Formal :** In Flat Organisation Structure, a manager has to manage many subordinates. Therefore, the relationship between them will be formal. **Control :** In Flat Organization Structure, there is a loose control because there are many subordinates. **Mistake :** In Flat Organization Structure, many mistakes may occur because of loose supervision and control. **Discipline :** In Flat Organization Structure, the possibility of indiscipline exists because there are many subordinates. **Cost :** Flat Organization Structure is less costly because it has less managers. **Process :** In Flat Organization Structure, Decision making and Communication is quick because there are few levels of management.

Que : When a matrix structure can be used ? (Manager in matrix type of organization)	Que : Explain New Forms of Organization Virtual and Self Organizing Systems.
Matrix organization is a hybrid structure. Matrix Organization is a combination of two or more organization structures. For example, Functional Organization and Project Organization.

The organization is divided into different functions, e.g. Purchase, Production, R & D, etc. Each function has a Functional (Departmental) Manager, e.g. Purchase Manager, Production Manager, etc.

The organization is also divided on the basis of projects e.g. Project A, Project B, etc. Each project has a Project Manager e.g. Project A Manager, Project B Manager, etc. The employee has to work under two authorities (bosses). The authority of the Functional Manager flows downwards while the authority of the Project Manager flows across (side wards). So, the authority flows downwards and across. Therefore, it is called "Matrix Organization".

Functional Manager : The Functional Manager has authority over the technical (functional) aspects of the project.

Project Manager : The Project manager has authority over the administrative aspects of the project. He has full authority over the financial and physical resources which he can use for completing the project.

For example, all engineers may be in one engineering department and report to an engineering manager but these same engineers may be assigned to different projects and report to a project manager while working on that project. Therefore each engineer may have to work under several managers to get their job done.

Advantages of Matrix Organization
- Sound Decisions
- Development of Skills
- Top Management can concentrate on Strategic Planning : Responds to Changes in Environment
- Specialization
- Optimum Utilization of Resources
- Motivation

Limitations of Matrix Organization
- Increase in Work Load
- High Operational
- Absence of Unity of Command
- Difficulty of Balance
- Power Struggle
- Morale
- Complexity
- Shifting of Responsibility | **Virtual Organization**

You might ask yourself the question "Why do we need to go to a specific physical place to work?"

The answer often is that either "this is where the people that you work with are" or "that this is where you find the information you need as well as the means to process it"- in summary where your office is.

But what if you no longer had to go to this place to contact the people or get the information? Instead all this could be done electronically and you and everyone else would do their work from any location. In that case you can have taken the first few steps to a virtual organization.

A Virtual org. is a network of firm held together by the product. A Virtual Org. might not have even have a permanent office. For example, *"John Taylor"* is a renowned company. When you try to track down the John Taylor company, you find there are no John Tyalor designers, no John Taylor manufactures. It is just 3 people in an office subcontracting out all functions.

A virtual organization consists a group of companies, acting as one company to fulfill a need in the marketplace. These companies collaborate, share skills, information, products, services etc in order to meet the goal of customer fulfillment. Indeed, a company can itself be a virtual enterprise consisting of interdependent departments. These companies operate independently of each other but work together to meet a common goal of meeting a need in the market.

A virtual organization or company is one whose members are geographically apart, usually working by computer e-mail and groupware while appearing to others to be a single, unified organization with a real physical location.

Self-Organizing Systems

Self-organizing systems are to put in simple manner – the system whose parts are separate, independent of each other, and then these parts acts in such a way that they form connections with each other. Thus, this system is a system that emerges from "independent parts" to interdependent parts" of the system.

In other words these systems can be considered as spontaneous interconnecting systems. |

Que : Explain Formalization, Work Specialization & Chain of Command	Que : Explain types of Organizational Structure.
Formalization Formalization refers to how standardized an organization's jobs are and the extent to which employee behavior is guide by rules and procedures. In highly formalized organizations, there are explicit jobs descriptions, numerous organizational rules, and clearly defined procedures covering work processes. Employees have little discretion over what's done, when it's done, and how it's done. However where formalization is low, employees have more discretion in how they do their work. **Work Specialization** It is also known as division of labor. An organization is composed of man power of different specialization or skills. So there should be proper division of work among different workers. **Advantages** :- 1. Increase in production rate. 2. Quality of product is better. • **Disadvantages** :- 1. Workers may lose interest due to repetition of jobs. 2. Workers may not get change for job enlargement. 3.Work becomes boredom & chances of absenteeism increased & reduced performance. **Chain of command** It is the line of authority extending from upper organizational levels to lower levels, which clarifies who reports to whom. Mangers need to consider it when organizing work because it helps employees with questions such as "Who do I report to?" and " Who do I go to if I have a problem?" **1. Authority** :- It refers to the rights inherent in a managerial position to tell people what to do and to expect them to do it. Authority empowers the superior to make a subordinate to do the work. Lines of authority should be clearly established in the structure of organization in order to avoid overlapping actions. **2. Responsibility** :- A manager assign work to employees & these employees has to perform the assigned duties. This obligation is known as responsibility. **3. Unity of Command** :- It states that a person should report to only one manager, without unity of command it creates confusion & problems.	**If this question will be asked, Types of organization (Line, Functional, Staff etc) should be written to avoid confusion.** There are three main types of organizational structure: functional, divisional and matrix structure. **Functional Structure** Functional structure is set up so that each portion of the organization is grouped according to its purpose. In this type of organization, for example, there may be a marketing department, a sales department and a production department. The functional structure works very well for small businesses in which each department can rely on the talent and knowledge of its workers and support itself. However, one of the drawbacks to a functional structure is that the coordination and communication between departments can be restricted by the organizational boundaries of having the various departments working separately. **Divisional Structure** Divisional structure typically is used in larger companies that operate in a wide geographic area or that have separate smaller organizations within the umbrella group to cover different types of products or market areas. For example, the now-defunct Tecumseh Products Company was organized divisionally--with a small engine division, a compressor division, a parts division and divisions for each geographic area to handle specific needs. The benefit of this structure is that needs can be met more rapidly and more specifically; however, communication is inhibited because employees in different divisions are not working together. Divisional structure is costly because of its size and scope. Small businesses can use a divisional structure on a smaller scale, having different offices in different parts of the city, for example, or assigning different sales teams to handle different geographic areas. **Matrix Structure** The third main type of organizational structure, called the matrix structure, is a hybrid of divisional and functional structure. Typically used in large multinational companies, the matrix structure allows for the benefits of functional and divisional structures to exist in one organization. This can create power struggles because most areas of the company will have a dual management--a functional manager and a product or divisional manager working at the same level and covering some of the same managerial territory.

Unit - 5 : Organizational Culture and Environment

Que : Define Organizational Culture. Explain the attributes of organizational culture.
Que : What factors affect the relative ease of managing organizational culture ?
Que : Describe how culture is transmitted to employees.
Que : Describe seven dimensions of organizational culture.
Que : What roles does culture play in organization and to employees ?

Culture is a set of values and beliefs that has been defined by community and society. *Organizational culture is a system of shared beliefs, values, assumptions and rituals which has been defined by organizational people.*

Every organization has a culture. The norms of this culture are not written. You can sense it, feel it but you cannot see Organizational Culture. Corporate culture can be looked at as a system. At the surface level, culture can be visible in symbols, slogans, languages, behaviors, histories and stories, dress codes rituals and ceremonies. But actually it is associated with objectives and functions. Do not expect your organization culture to be easily changed by switching your logos, rearranging the layout of your office space.

The success or failure of an organization is attributed to the prevailing culture in organization. The organizational culture is largely articulated with reference to the prevailing internal and external environment. The environement refers to the forces that affect the organizational performance. The environment are basically classified into two categories : (1) Internal (2) External

   (1) Internal Environment refers to the factors which are within the organization and are controllable by managerial decisions and action.
   (2) External Environment refers to factors and forces outside the organization which affect the organization's performance.

According to Eliott Jacques, an organizational culture is 'the custom or traditional ways of thinking and doing things…" In other words, Organizational culture is a framework that guide day to day behavior and decision making for employees and directs their actions towards completion of organizational jobs.

There are two levels of culture : One visible and one invisible. First, on the visible level, are the behavior patterns and styles of the employees. Second, on the invisible level, are the shared values and assumptions. This second level is the more difficult to change.

When employees join an organization, the manager introduces them to culture of the organization during training sessions or during interviews. Through words and actions the manager conveys the written and unwritten rules that all employees must follow. Company's slogans, architecture of a company's building and grounds can reflect its corporate culture.

Some illustrative organizational culture is presented :

   (1) Mind Tree, a global IT firm posses a strong passion for custom satisfaction.
   (2) IBM emphasized the team work approached by employees.
   (3) Vijay Mallya's lavish lifestyle influenced him to provide excellent facility to passengers in his airline Kingfisher.
   (4) Kuman Manglam, Birla Group and Dhirubhai Ambani of Ambani Group always drew best talent in respective field.
   (5) Nirma's founder Karshanbhai Patel followed risk taking appetite.

Seven Dimensions / Attributes of Culture

(1) Innovation and Risk Taking : Risk and returns go hand in hand. Places where you take a risk (calculated risk of course!), the chances of returns are higher

(2) Outcome Orientation : Some organizations pay more attention to results rather than processes.

(3) People Orientation : Some organizations are famous for being employee oriented as they focus more on creating a better work environment for its 'associates' to work in. Others still are feudal in nature, treating employees no better than work-machines.

(4) Team Orientation : It is a well-established fact today that synergistic teams help give better results as compared to individual efforts. Each organization makes its efforts to create teams that will have complementary skills and will effectively work together.

(5) Stability : While some organizations believe that constant change and innovation is the key to their growth, others are more focused on making themselves and their operations stable. The managements of these organizations are looking at ensuring stability of the company rather than looking at indiscriminate growth.

(6) Attention to Detail : It is the degree of the details employees are expected to exhibit the precision and analysis.

(7) Aggressiveness : It is the degree to which employees in organization are aggressive and competititive rather than mild and co-operative.

Que: "Change is crucial for the survival of a business organization."	Que : Explain the change process. OR Lewin's model of change process
Things are neither created nor destroyed really. They only change their forms. Change crucial for human life. What is true for human life is also true for organizations. An organization is like a living organism. Organization survival is dependent on a series of exchange with external environment. If any change occurs in external environment, organization must change according to change in external environment. The company must update with the outside world by adaptations such as changing marketing strategy, bringing in new product range, revamping its organizational structure, manufacturing technologies and locations. Research has proved very interesting findings : (1) Average life span of a corporations is much shorter than its potential life span (2) The average corporate life expectancy is less than 50 years (3) There are a few successful companies with age ranging from 100 to 700 years. There are few companies, among successful living companies, who have faced the challenges of change during the Middle Ages, the Reformation, the wars, the Industrial Revoultion and the two world wars. These long living companies survive and exists in a world that they have no control over, the world is highly unstable and very difficult to influence in any way. This is possible only when the companies are willing to adapt to the change. For example. Lloyd and IBM are the best examples who have lived for many years. Over 300 years ago, Lloyd's started out in Edward Lloyd's coffee house as a place where ship owners and merchants could meet with financiers to discuss ways to match the risks they faced at sea with the capital they needed to insure them. The world has changed a lot in 300 years, but no matter what social, political or economic changes have taken place, Lloyd's has always provided new types of insurance to meet new needs. Lolyd insured the first motorcars in the UK and we were also involved in insuring the first ever commercial space flights. In brief, the organizations which manage the change and adapt themselves to the change effectively only stand a better chance of living longer. Everything has birth, growth and decay. Old things ultimately give way to new ones. Just as Human , Companies are also facing the problem of decay and death. If any organization is compatible with changes, it will live up to many years.	Change is a common thread that runs through all businesses regardless of size, industry and age. One of the cornerstone models for understanding organizational change was developed by Kurt Lewin back in the 1950s, and still holds true today. His model is known as ***Unfreeze Change Refreeze***, refers to the three-stage process of change he describes. If you have a large cube of ice, but realize that what you want is a cone of ice, what do you do? First you must melt the ice to make it amenable to change (unfreeze). Then you must mold the iced water into the shape you want (change). Finally, you must solidify the new shape (refreeze).  **Cube of Ice** **Cone of Ice** **(1) Unfreeze :** This first stage of change involves preparing the organization to accept that change is necessary, which involves break down the existing status quo before you can build up a new way of operating. This first part of the change process is usually the most difficult and stressful. When you start cutting down the "way things are done", you put everyone and everything off balance. It may evoke strong reactions / oppositions in people, and that exactly what needs to be done **(2) Change :** After the uncertainty created in the unfreeze stage, the change stage is where people begin to resolve their uncertainty and look for new ways to do things. People start to believe and act in ways that support the new direction. The transition from unfreeze to change does not happen overnight: People take time to embrace the new direction and participate proactively in the change. In order to accept the change and contribute to making the change successful, people need to understand how the changes will benefit them. Not everyone will fall in line just because the change is necessary and will benefit the company. **(3) Refreeze :** When the changes are taking shape and people have embraced the new ways of working, the organization is ready to refreeze. As part of the Refreezing process, make sure that you celebrate the success of the change this helps people to find closure, thanks them for enduring a painful time, and helps them believe that future change will be successful.

Que : Explain formal and informal groups. State of advantages and disadvantages of Informal Group.	Que : Write a note on internal and external environment.

BEST ANSWER CAN BE FOUND IN UNIT -1

Formal groups are official and rational structure. It depends on authority, responsibility and accountability while Informal organization are groups (networks) of people formed spontaneously. It is based upon social instincts, friendship, shared attitudes, interests, culture, linguistic and regional similarities.

Historically, some have regarded the informal organization as the byproduct of insufficient formal organization.

Advantage of Informal Group

(1) Social Status and Satisfaction : Informal groups provides social status and satisfaction which may not be ontained from the formal organization. Members of informal groups shares jokes, gripes, eat together, play and work together and are friend which contributes to personal esteem.

(2) Communication Channel : The informal group develops a communication channel (known as grapevine) to keep its memebers informed about what management actions will affect them in various ways.

(3) Social Control : They provide social control by influencing and regulating behavior inside and outside group.

Disadvantages of Informal Group

(1) Role Conflict : The quest for informal group satisafaction may lead memebers away from formal organizational objectives. What is good for and desired by informal group memebers is not always good for the organization. For example, Students by bunking the class and spending time with friends completes objectives of informal group but at the cost of study which is formal objective.

(2) Rumor : "Grapevine Communication" and "Rumor" are product of informal group. This can create problems for employees. Suppose one informal group is jealous about one employee. They will try to spoil image of that employees by spreading rumor. Rumor can be heard as genuine news as it was told by group.

Benefits of Informal Organization

- Blend with formal system
- Lighten management workload
- Fill gaps in management abilities

The environment refers to the forces that affect the organizational performance. The environment are basically classified into two categories.

(1) INTERNAL ENVIRONMENT refers to the factors which are within the organization and are controllable by managerial decisions and action. They include (i) technology know how (ii) manufacturing know-how (iii) marketing know-how (iv) distribution know-how (v) logistics know -how

(2) EXTERNAL ENVIRONMENT refers to factors and forces outside the organization that affect the organization's performance.

EXTERNAL ENVIRONMENT are further classified into two categories :

(a) Specific External Environment – Economic, Social, Political, Legal ,Technological, Global

(b) General External Environment – Customers, Suppliers, Competitors, Public Pressure

The environment which affects the managerial performance can be stable and dynamic. The degree of change in such environment and its impact on managerial performance is presented below :

Stable

(1) Stable and predictive environment. It is less complex.

(2) Competitors are few in number.

(3) Minimum need for mastering sophisticated knowledge of components.

Dynamic

(1) Dynamic and unpredictable environment.

(2) Competitors are large in number.

(3) Maximum need for mastering sophisticated knowledge of quick adjustments to changing environment.

Que : Explain Organizational Behavior & Models of Organizational Behavior	Que : Strong and Weak Culture. Types of Organizational Culture

Que : Explain Organizational Behavior & Models of Organizational Behavior

Behaviour is actions of individual in a given environmental situation and organization. Organizational behavior is study of how people behave within organizations as individuals and as groups.

Organizational behavior is systematic study of how behavior of the people individuals as well as groups is and how it is affected while working for and within an organization. Organization behavior is systematic body of behavior of individuals and groups with organizations and how organizational members and their external environment influence each other

Study of organization behavior enables individual to better understand his organizational roles and responsibilities and position. Study of organizational behavior helps individuals in understanding stress and encourages them to find ways to cope with it effectively.

Models of Organizational Behaviour

(1) Autocratic Model : All the powers are bested in one person or a few person. All affairs of business and people are governed by orders, rules and regulations. This model can be correlated to following theories :
McGregor's Theory X, Maslow's Hierarchy of Needs.

(2) Custodial Model : In this model , economic resources of the organization are a driving force and a chief concern of the organization. Employee depends on the organization for security and welfare. This model can be correlated to following theories :
Maslow's Hierarchy of Needs, Managerial Grid Theory

(3) Supportive Model : Leadership is a predominant force. Employees are well motivated and enjoy support from their leaders and managers while working, solving problems, facing hurdles and taking on bigger challenges. This model can be correlated to following theories :
McGregor's Theory Y, Maslow's Hierarchy of Needs.

(4) Collegial Model : This Model values employee needs and wants. It respects dignity of human beings. This model can be correlated to following theories :
Maslow's Hierarchy of Needs, Managerial Grid Theory

(5) S-O-B-C Model : Organizational Behavior is influenced by several internal and external factors. "S" means Situation, "O" means Organizm, "B" means Behavior and "C" means consequences

S ⟷ O ⟷ B ⟷ C

Que : Strong and Weak Culture. Types of Organizational Culture

Strong Culture

- Culture in which key values are deeply and widely held is called Strong Culture.
- Strong cultures have a strong influence on organizational members.
- Employees are more loyal organizations with strong culture (rate of employee turnover is less).
- Organizations with strong culture have shown better performance.
- In organizations with strong culture, most employees can tell stories about company history / heroes.
- Employees have clarity of cultural values (are very clear about the culture).
- One drawback (disadvantage) of strong culture is that employees may not try new approaches, especially when conditions are changing rapidly.

FACTORS INFLUENCING THE STRENGTH OF CULTURE

- **Size of the organization.**
- **Age of the organization.**
- **Rate of employee turnover.**
- **Strength of the original culture.**
- **Clarity of cultural values and beliefs.**

STRONG CULTURE

1) **Employees are more loyal in organizations with strong culture.**
2) **Organizations with strong culture have shown better performance.**
3) **Employees have clarity about the organizational culture.**
4) **Values widely shared.**

WEAK CULTURE

1) **Employees are less loyal in organizations with weak culture.**
2) **Performance of organizations with weak culture is not as good as the organizations with strong culture.**
3) **Employees are not clear about the Organizational culture.**
4) **Values limited to a few people – usually top management.**

Que : What is organization ? Write a note on principles of organization.	Que : Explain requirements of a sound organization.
"Organization is a system of co-operative activities of two or more persons." Organization is essentially a matter of relationship of man to man, job to job and department to department. Organization is the process of dividing up of the activities which are necessary to any purpose and arranging them in groups which are assigned to individuals. Organization is necessary for attaining maximum efficiency with minimum of resources. **Unity of Objectives** : The organization should be shaped to achieve its objectives. It implies that the structure of organization should be goal-orineted. **Efficiency** : The principle of efficiency must be observed in formation of organizational structure. The organization can maintain efficiency by minimum waste of resource. **Span of Control** : This principle takes into consideration maximum number of subordinates that a superior can supervise. **Scalar Principle and Delegation** : In any organization, final authority should be located at a definite point. There must be a clear line of authority running from top to bottom. If a person finds himself overburdened, he should assign some of his duties to some other persons in the organization. **Authority and Responsibility** : Responsibilities can be fulfilled in a better way if there is a proper balance between authority and responsibility. **Unity of Command** : This principle was put forth by Fayol. According to this principle , each employee should receive order only from one superior. **Departmentation** : Total activity of business unit should be divided into different departments, so that its objectives may be realized efficiently. **Balance** : The principle of balance should be followed, to establish a balance between different departments of the organization. **Leadership** : The structure of organization should be shaped that the manager gets opportunities to develop his leadership qualities and to use his capacity as a leader in business. **Continuity** : The principle implies that efficiency of an organization must not be highly dependent on any single person.	**Setting Objectives** : Any business unit or institution is established to attain certain specific objectives. The first step in forming organization is to decide clear objective of the enterprise. **Determination of Activities** : The next step is to determine activities needed to execute the plans as per the objectives of the unit. **Grouping Activities** : Once the major activities are listed, they are grouped as per their functional characteristics. **Setting Authorities and Responsibilities** : After grouping, activites are given status as important and ordinary activities. Authoirty and Responsibility are set up at each level of activity. This will decide "Superior-subordinate" relationship. **Establishing Inter-relationships** : Activities at different levels needs to be integrated for coordinated efforts towards common goal achievement. **Preparing Organization Chart** : This is concluding step in formation of an organization. It is graphical representation of formal organization structure showing positions of management, staff and their relationship. **Extra : Out of Syllabus Question** **Schein's Three Levels of Culture** Schein has suggested three levels of culture. These three levels of culture are also called as basic elements of culture. The three basic elements of organizational culture (3 levels of culture) are **ARTIFACTS** : Artifacts are things that "one sees, hears, and feels". It includes products, services, and behaviors of group members. Artifacts are everywhere so we can see, hear or feel them. **ESPOUSED VALUES** : Espoused values are the values that we want to promote and adopt in the organization. These are the reasons that we give for doing what we do. **BASIC ASSUMPTIONS** : These are the beliefs and assumptions that members take for granted. Certain values are assumed (taken for granted) by the members of the organization. These are unspoken assumptions

Unit - 5 : Social Responsibility and Managerial Ethics

Que : How ethics and social responsibility play role in management ?
Que : Explain the 'social responsibility' of a business.
Que : Define Corporate Social Responsibility and state its characteristics.
State the evolution of corporate social responsibility.

Social responsibility means eliminating corrupt, irresponsible or unethical behavior which might bring harm to the community, its people and the environment.

Organization survival is dependent upon a series of exchanges between the organization and its environment. If you are doing something for external environment, that means you are doing something for your own organization. For example , if you want to set up Computer Manufacturing Company in tribal country, then you need to provide education to tribal people. On the contrary, you are doing work for your own organization.

Social responsibility is voluntary. It is about going above and beyond what is called for by the law. The concept of social responsibility is fundamental an ethical concept.

Organizations are the part of the society. It operates within society. It utilizes resources of society like water, electricity , etc. Because of this, they need to pay for this obligation. Business is no longer a mere occupation, it is an economic institution operating in social environment.

Why should Business be social responsible ?

(1) <u>Public Image</u> - The activities of business towards the welfare of the society earn goodwill and reputation for the business. The earnings of business also depend upon the public image of its activities. People prefer to buy products of a company that engages itself in various social welfare programmes. Again, good public image also attracts honest and competent employees to work with such employers.

(2) <u>Government Regulation</u> :   To avoid government regulations businessmen should discharge their duties voluntarily. For example, if any burn:-firm pollutes the environment it will naturally come under strict government regulation which may ultimately force the firm to close down its business. Instead, the business firm should engage itself in maintaining a pollution free environment.

(3) <u>Survival and Growth</u> : Every business is a part of the society. So for its survival and growth, support from the society is very much essential. Business utilizes the available resources like land, water, electricity of

the society- So it should be the responsibility of every business to spend a part of its profit for the welfare of the society.

(4) <u>Employee Satisfaction</u> : Employees are the part of society. If you satisfy their needs, then you are doing social work. Besides getting good salary and working in a healthy atmosphere, employees also expect other facilities like proper accommodation, transportation, education and training. The employers should try to fulfill all the expectations of the employees because employee satisfaction is directly related to productivity and it is also required for the long-term prosperity of the organization. For example, if business spends money on training of the employees, it will have more efficient people to work and thus, earn more profit.

(5) <u>Consumer Awareness</u> : Now-a-days consumers have become very conscious about their rights. They protest against the supply of inferior and harmful products by forming different groups. This has made it obligatory for the business to protect the interest of the consumers by providing quality products at the most competitive price If you are giving higher quality products at cheap rate, that is one kind of social responsibility.

Principles of corporate social responsibility

(1) The *charity principle* required the more fortunate members of society to assist its less fortunate members including the unemployed, the handicapped, the sick and the elderly.

(2) The *stewardship principle* derived from the Bible , required businesses and wealthy individuals to view themselves as the stewards or caretakers of their property.

Milton Friedman argued that manger's primary responsibility is to operate the business in the best interests of the stockholders , whose primary concerns are financial.

Ethics is simply the rule that say what is right and wrong as defined by a particular reference group or individual. Use of Company Car for Private Use is unethical thing. Ethics can be defined as the principles , values and beliefs that define right and wrong decision's and behavior.

(Contid...)

Managing Ethical Lapses and Social Irresponsibility

Behavior of employees like failing asleep at work, spreading rumor about a co-worker, snooping after hours are becoming serious concern for managers. Manager can tackle this situation by two ways – by ethical leadership and protection of those who report wrongdoing.

Ethical Leadership : It is the belief that what managers do has a strong influence on employees. If manager cheats, lies, steals or manipulates, then they are sending wrong signals to employees.

Protection of employees who raise ethical issues : Some persons in company informs managers about unethical practice. It is manager's duty to protect those types of employees. Managers also need to create a culture where bad news can be heard and acted on before it's too late.

Social Entrepreneurship

A Social Entrepreneur is an individual or organization who seeks out opportunities to improve society by using practical, innovative and sustainable approaches. Social Entrepreneurs want to make the world a better place.

Samsung Galaxy Note has started social movement, "Purchase Galaxy Note and Give Note to Poor Childern" to give education to less fortunate children of society.

Devi Prasad Shetty founded Narayana Hrudayalaya Hospital in Banglore in 2001. These hospitals perform 32 heart surgeries a day. 60 % of the treatments are provided below cost or for free. Since the last three decades, HDFC contributes 7 % of its income to support community needs. Mahindra Tech employees donated one day salary to help victims of Bihari floods. Wipro has set up a foundation named Azim Premji Foundation to help improve education of the elementary schools in rural India. Satyam encourages its employees to volunteer his/her time for its social projects like Emergency 108 numbers. Brooke Bond has been interested in animal welfare, providing veterinary service.

Green Management

Managers and Organizations can do many things to protect and preserve the natural environment. The Plastic shopping bags – An ugly symbol of development. Some 110 billions are used each year in world and only 2 % of those bags are recycled. Plastic shopping bags can last 1000 years in landfills. Some companies are not in favour of plastic bags.

For example, IKEA encourages customers to use fewer bags by charging a nickel. Many stores such as Fab India and Colour Plus only gives paper bags. The largest solar steam cooking system for 15000 persons per day has been set up at Tirupati Tirumala Devsthanam. India's largest tyre company, MRF has recently launched a new tubeless, eco-friendly rubber tyre that reduces rolling resistance and results in lower fuel consumption. Bajaj Auto has installed wind power generation units in three factories which saves Rs. 25 crore in power costs every year. The Orchid Ecotel Hotel – Asia's first eco-friendly 5 star hotel chain is conserving natural resources without compromising quality of service.

Social Stakeholders

The primary responsibility of a business is to protect the interests of its shareholders. The shareholders provide the core resources – the capital – that enables an organization to operate and grow. Shareholders should be provided with adequate and timely information about functioning of the organization.

Stockholder and Stakeholder View Points

The *stockholder viewpoint* of social responsibility is the traditional perspective. It believes that business firms are responsible only to their owners and stockholders. The job of managers is therefore to satisfy the financial interests of the stockholders. Socially irresponsible acts ultimately result in poor sales. According to the stockholder point of view, corporate social responsibility is a by product of profit seeking.

The *stakeholder viewpoint* of social responsibility contends that firm must hold themselves responsible for the quality of life of the many groups affected by the firm's actions. These interested parties or stakeholders include those groups composing the firm's general environment. Two categories of stakeholders exist. Internal stakeholders include owners, employees and stockholders; external stakeholders include customers, labor unions, consumer groups and financial institutions. The stakeholder viewpoint reflects the modern viewpoint of the corporation.

Many organizations regard their various stakeholders as partner in achieving success. The organization and the stakeholders work together for their mutual success. For example, Ford Motor Company owns 49 % of Hertz rental car company, which is also a major Ford Company. Ford Company is facing financial troubles in recent years, a mutual relationship of this type is essential.

Thus, Ethics and Social responsibility plays major role in management.

Que : State and explain the myths about business ethics.	Que : State the guideline for managing ethics in the workplace.
The concept of the ethics is based on the philosophy and psychological parameters.	Ethics is simply the rule that say what is right and wrong as defined by a particular reference group or individual. Ethics can be defined as the principles, values and beliefs that define right and wrong decisions and behavior. Ethics stems from the personal behavior of an individual. Ethics is set of rules and standards that guide the individual or group behavior.
(1) It is difficult to apply ethics. : Many managers believe that ethics cannot be managed. At the most organization can make rules and regulation to keep on the ethical behavior of employees.	
(2) There is need for ethical policy as all our employees are ethical. : Most of the managers believe that since everything is going on well, all the employees are doing their jobs ethically.	The business ethics are broadly classified into (i) Personal Ethics (ii) Professional Ethics (iii) Managerial Ethics
(3) Since Ethics is a complex matter, academicians and philosophers can be best people to understand it. : Managers and leaders in organizations have shown less interest in it and left the interpretation to academicians and philosophers.	(i) Personal Ethics refers to the individual beliefs and the backed up behavior when they show the concern for others. (ii) Professional ethics refers the adherence to the set rules and standards for the good of all. (iii) Managerial ethics refers to the behavior of the mangers who are authorized by the promoter of the organization.
(4) Business Ethics is a new fashion : Many managers believe that since the concept of management ethics has found place in B-schools and other literature, it is fashion to speak about the same.	The business ethics are described under different approaches (i) the legal approach (ii) the market approach (iii) the stakeholders approach (iv) the activist approach
(5) Since we follow all laws, we are ethical : Organization which follow all the rules and regulations believe that they are ethical.	(i) The legal approach refers to the acts and behavior required under the formal rules and regulations. (ii) The market approach refers to concerns of business organizations to become more sensitive to the environmental issues.
(6) Ethics is related to religion and business has nothing to do with religion. This is a wrong perception about ethics.	(iii) The stakeholders approach shows the concern of business organizations towards the interests of internal stakeholders like managers and employees and also of external stakeholders like customers, suppliers, competitors.
(7) Ethics is philosophical, theological and academic in nature. It has very little pragmatic application. This is a wrong and narrow conception of business affairs.	(iv) The activist approach refers to the protection of the earth's resources like sun, air, water, and climate.
(8) Ethics is superfluous (unnecessary) and indicates only showiness to outside world. In fact, business ethics is based on the role of the organization in a social system.	Guideline for Managing Ethics in Workplace
(9) It is believed that business ethics and social responsibilities of the business mean the same thing. In fact, there is a technical differences between two concepts. Business ethics deals with governing the corporate behavior towards social responsibilities.	(1) Think before you act (2) Ask yourself "what if " questions (3) Seek opinions form others (4) Do what you truly believe is right (5) Encouraging Ethical Behavior (6) Employee Selection (7) Job Goals and Performance Appraisal (8) Ethics Training
(10) It is believed that ethics is internal and has an individual perception and so it is not amenable for managing control.	(9) Know your organization's policy on ethics (10) Codes of Ethics and Decision Rules (11) Understand the ethics policy

Que : Discuss factors that affect managerial ethics.	Que : Discuss the concept of ethics. What issues must a manager consider when applying ethics ?
Ethics is simply the rule that say what is right and wrong as defined by a particular reference group or individual. Ethics can be defined as the principles, values and beliefs that define right and wrong decisions and behavior. Ethics stems from the personal behavior of an individual. Ethics is related to Moral Development. There are three levels of moral development. The Idea of Moral development is based on internal values, and less dependent on outside factors.	Ethics is simply the rule that say what is right and wrong as defined by a particular reference group or individual. Ethics can be defined as the principles, values and beliefs that define right and wrong decisions and behavior. The Websters Dictionary defines ethics as "Ethics relates to what is good or bad, and it deals with moral duty and obligation." Ethics implies the conformity with the code of conduct. A business unit can be treated with a ripple effect like company, industry, national economy and finally global economy.

MORAL DEVELOPMENT

1. <u>Preconventional Level</u> : A Person's Choice between right and wrong is based on personal consequences from outside sources such as physical punishment, reward and exchange of favors. Authority, Punishment, Fear of Boss prevents employee to practice unethical things.
- Strict to rules to avoid punishment

2. <u>Conventional Level</u> : Ethical decisions rely on maintaining expected standards and living up to the expectations of others. For example, Students often think about to bunk class but syllabus fear will prevent him from doing this thing repeatedly.
- Live upto what is expected by people close to you

3. <u>Principles Level</u> : An individual has their own moral values and principles which prevents him from doing any unethical task.
- Follow self-chosen ethical principles even if they violate the law

INDIVIDUAL CHARACTERISTICS

Our values develop from a young age, from upbringing, from family; from college and school education also affect managerial ethics.

Ego Strength and Locus of Control also plays major role in managerial ethics. People with high ego are likely to resist impulses to act unethically. Locus of control is the degree to which people believe they control their own fate.

ORGANISATION'S CULTURE

An organization's structural design can influence behaviors of an employee. An Organizational Culture also encourages ethical behavior.

Thus, managers have to understand the above mentioned factors that influence their decisions.

MAINTENANCE OF ENVIRONMENT

- Clean-up existing pollution
- Controlling noise pollution
- Control the use of limited land resources

CONSUMERS

- Fair and transparent deals through advertisement and consumer education
- Control on harmful products

COMMUNITY NEEDS

- Use business to solve social problems
- To help in education and health care
- To help in urban activities

GOVERNMENT

- To encourage new innovative regulation on business
- Avoidance of political lobbying

SOCIETY

- Financial support for development of human resources
- Financial support to socially desirable activities

MINORITIES

- To provide training and employment
- To provide preferred quota for minority employment

This is just extra information. Just move your eyes on this page.

<u>**Ethics Management Programs**</u> : Organizations can manager ethics in their workplaces by establishing an ethics management program. A corporate ethics program is made up of values, policies and activities which impact the propriety of organization behaviors.

<u>**Benefits of Managing Ethics as a Program**</u>

- Establish organizational roles to manage ethics
- Schedule ongoing assessment of ethics requirement
- Establish required operating values and behaviors
- Develop awareness and sensitivity to ethical issues
- Integrates ethical guidelines to decision making

<u>**Codes of Ethics**</u> : A code generally describes the highest values to which the company aspires to operate. A code of ethics specifies the ethical rules of oepartion. If an organization is quite large which includes several large departments, you may want to develop an orverall corporate code of ethics and then a separate code to guide each of your departments. The code should not be developed out of the Human Resource or Legal departments alone. All staff must see the ethics program being driven by top management.

<u>**Ethical Dilemma**</u> : Business ethics is portrayed as a matter of resolving conflicts in which one option is clear choice. An ethical dilemma exists when one is faced with having to make a choice among these alternatives.

<u>**Ethical Temptations and Violations**</u>
Certain ethical mistakes, including illegal actions, recur in the workplace. Familiarizing oneself with these behaviors can be helpful in managing the ethical behavior of others as well as monitoring one's own behavior.

- Stealing from employers and customers.

- Illegally copying software.

- Sexual harassment

- Accepting kickbacks and bribes for doing business with another company.

- Divulging confidential information

- Misuse of corporate resources

- Extracting extraordinary compensation from the organization

- Poor cyberethics.

<u>**Business Scandals as Ethical Violations**</u>

Major ethical and legal violations have long been a part of the business world. The best-known scandals are associated with infamous executives. Yet scandals including Internet fraud, identity theft, and work-at-home scams (such as making you an agent for transferring funds received from cus¬tomers) are perpetuated by players everywhere. Identity theft and virus spreading are rampant on Facebook and Twitter.

<u>**Click Fraud.**</u>
An individual or dozens of people click on Internet advertising solely to generate illegitimate revenue for the Web site carrying those ads. (Search engines charge the advertiser by the number of mouse clicks in response to an ad.) The people doing the clicking receive a small payment also. Major search engines such as Google and Yahoo! attempt to minimize click fraud, and the scandal usually focuses on a parked Web site. Nevertheless, a major search engine benefits from click fraud. A parked Web site usually has little or no content except for lists of Internet ads. Because Google and Yahoo! have distributed these ads to the parked sites, the scam artists receive a small cut of the money Google and Yahoo! receive from the advertiser. The owner of the parked Web site might use live people or software to generate an enormous number of useless clicks on the Web sites of advertisers. About 10 percent to 15 percent of ad clicks are estimated to be fake.

<u>**Enron Corporation**</u>

One of the most famous business frauds of all time was the collapse of Enron Corporation in 2001. Jeffrey Skilling was the last Enron executive to be punished; he was sent to prison for 24 years and four months. Accounting tricks and dishonest deals cost thousands of jobs, along with $60 billion in shareholder value and more than $2 billion in employee pension assets. Dawn Powers Martin, a 22-year Enron employee summed up years of testimony in these words: "Mr. Skilling has proved to be a liar, a thief and a drunk, flaunting an attitude above the law. He has betrayed everyone who trusted him."22 When Enron was on the rise, Skilling was considered to be a brilliant business strategist who had found new ways of making money for a corporation.

A person reading these examples of unethical manager behavior might wonder how wealthy, intelligent people could exercise such poor judgment. The answer lies partially in the explanations for unethical behavior presented earlier, with particular attention to greed, gluttony, and avarice.

Unit - 6 : Marketing Management

Different Concepts in Marketing

(1) THE PRODUCTION CONCEPT : This concept is the oldest of the concepts in business. It holds that consumers will prefer products that are widely available and highly affordable. Managers focusing on this concept concentrate on achieving high production efficiency, low costs, and mass distribution. We prefer "Nirma" Detergent, Wag Bakri Tea, Tata Salt & Amul Milk because it is affordable and available in the market.

(2) THE PRODUCT CONCEPT : This concept holds that customers will prefer products that offer the most in quality, performance and innovative feature. Product Quality and Improvements are important parts of marketing strategies. But Customers don't always want quality, they are much concerned about price. Suppose one company makes Digital Mouse Trap and sells it in Rs. 20000, nobody will buy it because there are many cheap options are available in the market.

(3) THE SELLING CONCEPT : This concept holds that consumers will only buy products if it takes large scale selling and promotion efforts. Recently one Gujarati movie named "Kevi Rite Jais" gained attention form the world. Traditional Gujarati Movie doesn't go for promotion and large scale selling. But, this movie was released in Multiplex Theatre at large scale with much promotion. The movie got success even in city areas.

(4) THE MARKETING CONCEPT : This concept holds that achieving organization goals depends on needs and wants of target markets and consumers. The company should be more effective competitors in creating, delivering, and communicating customer value to its selected target customers. Customer Needs and Wants are key factors in this concept. Southwest Airlines don't have marketing department; they have customer department.

(5) THE SOCIETAL MARKETING CONCEPT : This concepts focuses on conflicts between "short run wants" and "consumer long run welfare." This concepts holds that marketing strategy should deliver values to customers in a way that maintains or improves both consumers and society. Advertment of Mineral Water indicates that they are loving nature. But CO2 emission for Mineral Water Plant can cause danger to society. Mineral Water is a short term requirement but it has adverse effect on society because CO2 emission and wastage of plastic.

(5) THE HOLISTIC MARKETING CONCEPT : The holistic marketing concept is based on the development, design, and implementation of marketing programs. The holistic concept of marketing takes the global considerations in the marketing management.

Four "Ps" in Marketing – Marketing Mix

Jeorme MacCarthy in his book on "Basic Marketing - A Managerial Approach" has identified following 4Ps of maketing which are popularly known as marketing mix.

(1) PRODUCT : Product means a good idea, method, information ,objects & service. A Product is defined as " a bundle of satisfaction." A product is a sum of product attributes like functional characteristics, aesthetic value, emotional value. It is interesting that all products are not accepted by the consumer. There are many products in the market which die soon. Gocool Icecream, Priya Soft Drinks, Goldspot have failed in Gujarat State while Vadilal Ice Cream, Rasna Soft Drink, 2-Minutes Nudles have been successfully marketed.

(2) PRICE : Price is the amount of money customers must pay to obtain the product. Price is a peculiar factor which depends on seller. For example, Tata Motors rarely charge the full sticker price. Instead they negotiate the price with each customer, offering discount etc. Major consideration in pricing is the costing of the product, the advertising and marketing expenses, any price fluctuations in the market, distribution costs etc.

(3) PLACE : Place includes company activities that make the product available to target consumers. There is always a physical distance between the point of production and point of sale. Place refers to the distribution channel of a product. If a product is a consumer product, it needs to be available as far and wide as possible. On the other hand, if the product is a Premium consumer product, it will be available only in select stores. Similarly, if the product is a business product, you need a team who interacts with businesses and makes the product available to them.

(4) PROMOTION : Promotion means activities that communicate the merits of products and convince customers to buy it. It focuses on the introduction of the new products, entering new markets, increasing the consumption of the existing new markets, grabbing a higher markets. It is basically a communication function with the present and potential customers generally through advertising media, media selection and advertisement.

What is Marketing ? Marketing vs Selling

Marketing is the performance of the business activities that direct the flow of goods and services from the producer (manufacturer) to consumer or end user. In short, Marketing defines a track form producer to consumers and brings products towards consumers. Marketing and Selling are two different things. Selling is subset of marketing. Marketing is a specialized activity directed towards bringing toghther a producer on one hand and a consumer or a buyer on the other. Marketing is used to identify the customer, satisfy the customer and keep the customer.

Marketing and Selling are two different things. Selling is a subset of marketing i.e. it is just a part of marketing.

(1) Marketing is broader concept which includes the product conception to the after sale services. Selling is a narrow concept and includes only the exchange of good between marketers and buyer.

(2) Marketing is a strategic higher level function while selling is an operational lower level function.

(3) Marketing functions are headed by the company marketing manager. The Selling functions are handled by the general sales managers.

(4) Marketing deals with product, price, place and promotion while selling basically focuses on place and promotion.

(5) The major part of the marketing process is pre-production in nature while Selling basically focuses on the post – production activities.

(6) Most of the marketing activities are related to the back office work. Most of the sales activities are carried out in the front office and in the outside field.

Method of Demand Forecasting

DEFINITION : It is the activity of estimating the quantity of a product or service that consumers will purchase. A demand forecast is the prediction of what will happen to your company's existing product sales.

IMPORTANCE OF DEMAND FORECASTING :
(1)   Planning and Scheduling Production
(2)   Budgeting of Costs and Sales Revenue
(3)   Making policies for long term
(4)   Planning of Finance
(5)   Planning of Labour
(6)   Continuous Supply of Commodities.

CRITERIA OF A GOOD FORECASTING METHOD :
(1)   Accuracy
(2)   Simplicity
(3)   Availability
(4)   Stability
(5)   Economy
(6)   Utility

METHODS OF DEMAND FORECASTING

(1)   SURVEY OF BUYER'S INTENTION (Consumer Market Survey)
Survey of Buyer's Intention is the most basic and the least sophisticated method. Customers plays an important role in estimating quantity. In this method, customers are asked about their purchase plans and buying behavior. The Customers are directly contacted for their intention to buy products. Their responses are recorded through personal interviews, mail or post service, telephone interviews and questionnaires. This method is simple to understand and easy to implement. This method is not suitable for long run because buyer's interests, willingness, intention is irregular and short term. If we have taken Buyer's Survey about Nokia's Phone Model in 2002, then it can not be used 2012. Because buyers interests is not constant for that particular product.
(2) SALES FORCE OPINION METHOD : In this method, Salesman plays an important role in estimating quantity. Since the salesperson is the one closest to the marketplace, he has the capacity to know what the customer wants. In this method, each salesperson is asked to project their sales.

(3) EXPERT OPINION METHOD / DELHI METHOD : The Delphi Method is a systematic, interactive method which relies on a panel of experts. A panel of expert will be formed. A panel of expert consists of an ordinary employee or an industry expert.

A questionnaire is carefully designed. The expert answers questionnaires in two or more rounds. All the answers are collected at central location. If answers are not similar, the round is once again organized. The process will be repeated until the final consent among members in the form of answer achieves.

(4) MARKET TEST METHOD : Introducing a new product is risky thing. In this method, companies develop a prototype model or description of the product or service that you can show to others. Best example is Famous Software Development Companies. Any antivirus software can introduce their product with demo (trial) version. Companies give free demo version of software for 30 days. By number of downloads or registrations, marketers can estimate the quantity of product. When trial or demo version is not available for product, companies creates prototype model or gives much priority to technical descriptions.

(5) TIME SERIES METHOD : Time Series Method uses a model to forecast future events based on known past events. Time Series Method is based only on past values. This method focuses on the influence of past and present data on future sales of your products. Suppose, 200000 pieces of Apple 2G was sold in 2006. 300000 pieces of Apple 3G was sold in 2010. By using past data, we can predict estimate quantity of Apple 4G.

(6) STATISTICAL DEMAND ANALYSIS : (CAUSAL MODEL) The Model uses a mathematical technique known as the regression analysis that relates a dependent variable (demand) to an independent variable (example, price, advertisement) in the form of a linear equation.

Extra Notes

(A) QUALITATIVE FORECASTING METHODS : This method doesn't depend on historical data or event. Survey of Buyer, Sales Force Opinion, Expert Opinion, Market Test Method are Qualitative Forecasting Methods.

(B) QUANTITATIVE FORECASTING METHODS : This method depends on historical data and events. Time series and Statistical Demand are quantitative Forecasting Methods

Market Segmentation. Bases for Consumer Market Segmentation

The Market consists of many types of customers, products and needs.

DEFINITION : The process of dividing a market into distinct group of buyers who have different needs, characteristics or behavior is called "Market Segmentation".

A Market Segment consists of group of customers who shares a similar set of needs and wants. There is difference between "mass marketing" and "segment marketing.". In mass marketing,, there is mass production, mass distribution and mass promotion. In Segment Marketing offers more benfits than mass marketing. The company can offer more defined products and market for consumers.

BASES / TYPES OF MARKET SEGMENTATION

(1) GEOGRAPHICAL SEGMENTATION : The division of the market into different geographical units such as nations, states, regions, countries, cities or neighborhoods. The major division in South Asia is the division of markets into rural and urban areas. Customer's interest, tastes and habits are totally different in different geographical units.For example, consumers in southern states like Tamil Nadu prefers coffee whereas consumers in many other states in India prefer tea. Even Some parts of India prefer strong tea whereas in some other parts, consumers prefer Nilgiri tea. Some parts of India prefer Air Coolers and some parts prefer AC because of dry and humid atmosphere.

(2) DEMOGRAPHIC SEGMENTATION : The division of market into groups on the basis of variables such as age, family, size, life cycle, gender, income, education , religion, nationality and social class. We have different products like Champak (Children), Playboy (Young Adults), Astha Channel (Aged People), Cartoon Network (Children), Fair and Handsome (Male), Fair and Lovely (Female) , Bajaj Wave (Women). These all products are example how market is divided on the basis of age, gender etc.

(3) PSYCHOGRAPHIC SEGMENTATION : The division of market into different groups on basis of psychological /personal traits, life styles or values. The best example is MacDonald. MacDonald's Burger in western country is made from Beef Mutton. But in India, because of religious issue, they are focusing on vegetarian products and chicken products. They are not using Beef Mutton. Many Restaurants have special defined dishes made from "Halal" and "Jhatka" mutton for Muslim and NonMuslims. Because "Halal" is authentic for Muslims. Muree Brewery are not making liquor (wine) in Muslim Countries. Because, Liquor is prohibited in Muslim Courtiers.
(4) BEHAVIORAL SEGMENTATION : In Behavioral Segmentation, marketers divide buyers into groups on the basis of knowledge of , attitude towards, use of or a response to a product. There are some products which are associated with some special occasions and benefits. For example, A Number of products such as Cadbury, Lays, Haldiram, Amul offer special gift pack for particular occasions. Cinthol, Dermi Cool , Navratna Oil is connected with benefits like coolness and freshness.

Product Life Cycle	Function of Packaging
Like Human beings, Products have a limited life. The four main stages of product life cycle are :	Packaging is the science, art and technology of enclosing or protecting products for distribution, storage, sale and use. Packing also refers to the process of design, evaluation and production of packages. Packaging contains protects, preserves, transports, informs and sells.

Product Life Cycle Curve

Product Life Cycle	Function of Packaging
(1) INTRODUCTION STAGE : At this stage, costs are very high. Slow sales volumes to start. Little or No Competition. Demand has to be created. Product makes no money at this stage.	(1) The objects enclosed in the package may require protection form mechanical shock, vibration, compression and temperature.
(2) GROWTH STAGE : Costs reduced due to economies of scale. Sales volumes increases. Profitability begins to rise. Competitors enters into market.	(2) To protect enclose content from oxygen, water, vapor, dust etc. Some packages contain Oxygen absorbers to help extend shelf life. Modified atmosphere or controlled atmosphere are also maintained in some food packages
(3) MATURITY STAGE : Costs are lowered. Sales Volume reaches at peak. Increase in Competitors. Industrial profits go down.	(3) Small Objects are typically grouped together in one package for reasons of efficiency. Single Pencil don't require box. But 10 pencils in one box can create convenience for handling and protection.
(4) DECLINE OR SATURATION STAGE : In this stage, products ends. Sales volume decline or stabilize. Profit is now challenge in this stage.	(4) Packages and Labels tells how to use, transport, recycle or dispose. It can also be used as a medium for marketing . The Graphic on Covers and Labels are used to encourage buyers to purchase the product
We have many examples like Bajaj Scooter, Kinetic , Kelvinator Freeze, Goldspot , Luna, Mobile Phones. These products are now history.	FUNCTIONS OF PACKAGING : • Protection • Advertisement • Promotion • Product Positioning • Identification • Convenience • Transportation • Counting

Segment Marketing

The Market consists of many types of customers, products and needs.

DEFINITION : The process of dividing a market into distinct group of buyers who have different needs, characteristics or behavior is called "Market Segmentation".

A Market Segment consists of group of customers who shares a similar set of needs and wants. There is difference between "mass marketing" and "segment marketing.". In mass marketing,, there is mass production, mass distribution and mass promotion. In Segment Marketing offers more benfits than mass marketing. The company can offer more defined products and market for consumers.

SEGMENT MARKETING

(1) NICHE MARKETING : A Niche is a defined group of customers who wants mix of benefits. Marketers identify niches by dividing a segment into sub segment. The best example is Colgate Tooth Cream. Previously we have only one white colour Colgate cream for all users. Now they have variants like Colgate Salt, Colgate Herb, Colgate Freshness for special defined niche.   In 1980s, there is only one channel "Doordarshan" which had all types of programs like news, sports, recipe show, entertainment and knowledge. Now for each well defined group, we have different particular individual channel like Star Sports, Astha, Zee Movies, Food Food, Star Cricket, News Channel. In Short, Niche marketing is done by taking care of special interest / special group of customers who wants more defined products from company.

(2) LOCAL MARKETING : Local Marketing is targeted to local audience. If fulfills needs and wants of local customers. Bharat Matrimony has local sites like Gujarati Matrimony, Bengali Matrimony etc targeted to local audience. Best Example is Spideman. . It was released in different Indian Languages like Bhojpuri etc to earn profit on local basis.

(3) INDIVIDUAL MARKETING : It is also known as "Customized Marketing" or "One to One Marketing". In this, products are prepared according to requirements and needs of Customers. Asian Paints Stores have colour machines. They will make colour tins by mixing colour according to the needs of customer. Gallleria Credit Card for United Bank, Pakistan gives a credit card which has your favorite photo on your card. Even Customize Burger is also best example of Individual Product.

Segment marketing is the practice of defining your customers needs and wants by placing them in specialized groups that receive different attention and different levels of marketing. The way customers are segmented by a company can vary from business to business but generally include areas such as income, regional location, sex, socioeconomic factors, and previous buying or business associations. Once the groups are designed, the object of segment marketing becomes unified; to offer customers marketing strategies and offers that are designed with their group characteristics in mind to produce profitable results for the company.

Market Research	Measures of Market Demand
Market research is any organized effort to gather information about markets or customers. It is a very important component of business strategy. The term is commonly interchanged with marketing research; however, expert practitioners may wish to draw a distinction, in that marketing research is concerned specifically about marketing processes, while market research is concerned specifically with markets Market research is for discovering what people want, need, or believe. It can also involve discovering how they act. Once that research is completed, it can be used to determine how to market your product. (1) MARKET INFORMATION : By Market information one can know the prices of different commodities in the market, as well as the supply and demand situation. (2) MARKET SEGMENTATION : Market segmentation is the division of the market or population into subgroups with similar motivations. (3) MARKET TRENDS : Market trends are the upward or downward movement of a market, during a period of time. The market size is more difficult to estimate if one is starting with something completely new. In this case, you will have to derive the figures from the number of potential customers, or customer segments	In the above listing, "product" refers to both physical products and services. The size of the market is not necessarily fixed. For example, the size of the available market for a product can be increased by decreasing the product's price, and the size of the qualified available market can be increased through changes in legislation that result in fewer restrictions on who can buy the product. Potential market - those in the total population who have interest in acquiring the product. Available market - those in the potential market who have enough money to buy the product. Qualified available market - those in the available market who legally are permitted to buy the product. Target market - the segment of the qualified available market that the firm has decided to serve (the served market). Penetrated market - those in the target market who have purchased the product.
Bases for Segmentation of Business Market	**Significance of Advertising in Marketing**
We can segment business markets with some of the same variable we use in cosumer markets, such as geography, benfits sought and usage rate but business marketers also use other variables A rubber tier company for example can sell tires to manufactures of automobiles, trucks , farm, tractors or aircraft. **Major Segmentation Varibale for Business Markets** (1) Demographic : Which industries should we serve ? What size companies should we serve ? What geographical areas should we serve ? (2) Operating Variables : What customer technologies should we focus on ? Should we servce heavy users, medium users, light users or nonusers ? (3) Purchasing Approaches : Should we serve companies with highly centralized or decentralized purchasing organization ? Should we serve companies that are seeking quality ? Service ? Price ? (4) Situational Factors : Should we serve companies that need quick and sudden delivery or service ? Should we focus on large or small orders ? (5) Personal Characteristics : Should we serve companies whose people and values are similar to ours ? Should we serve risk – taking or risk avoiding customers ? **Steps in Segmentation Process** • Need Based Segmentation • Segmentation Identification • Segment Attractiveness • Segment Profitability • Segment Positioning • Segment "Acid Test" • Marketing Mix Strategy	Advertising is the best way to communicate to the customers. Advertising helps informs the customers about the brands available in the market and the variety of products useful to them. Advertising is for everybody including kids, young and old. It is done using various media types, with different techniques and methods most suited. **Importance of Advertising** Advertising plays a very important role in today's age of competition. Advertising is one thing which has become a necessity for everybody in today's day to day life, be it the producer, the traders, or the customer. Advertising is an important part. Lets have a look on how and where is advertising important: (1) Advertising is important for the customers Just imagine television or a newspaper or a radio channel without an advertisement! No, no one can any day imagine this. Advertising plays a very important role in customers life. Customers are the people who buy the product only after they are made aware of the products available in the market. If the product is not advertised, no customer will come to know what products are available and will not buy the product even if the product was for their benefit. One more thing is that advertising helps people find the best products for themselves, their kids, and their family. When they come to know about the range of products, they are able to compare the products and buy so that they get what they desire after spending their valuable money. Thus, advertising is important for the customers. Advertising is important for the seller and companies producing the products (2) Advertising helps increasing sales Advertising helps producers or the companies to know their competitors and plan accordingly to meet up the level of competition.If any company wants to introduce or launch a new product in the market, advertising will make a ground for the product. Advertising helps making people aware of the new product so that the consumers come and try the product.Advertising helps creating goodwill for the company and gains customer loyalty after reaching a mature age. (3) Advertising is important for the society Advertising helps educating people. There are some social issues also which advertising deals with like child labour, liquor consumption, girl child killing, smoking, family planning education, etc. thus, advertising plays a very important role in society.

Unit - 7 : Financial Management

Meaning of Finance & Finance Management.	Scope of Finance Management
<ul><li>The Art and Science of Managing Money</li><li>A Branch of Economics concerned with resource allocation as well as resource management</li><li>A process of Decision Making</li><li>A Commercial Activity of providing funds and capital</li><li>The application of the planning and control functions to finance functions</li><li>The study of money or funds and how effectively they are allocated and utilized in business</li><li>Finance management is about how to buy, what to buy, when to buy and how to sell , what to sell and when to sell.</li></ul> **Types of Finance Needs in Business** LONG TERM FINANCIAL NEEDS : The Long Term needs are the requirements of funds for a period exceeding 5 – 10 year. For example, investment in plant , machinery, land , building etc are considered as long term finance. It is also known as long term capital or fixed capital. Larger manufacturing require more long term capital than small scale enterprises. MEDIUM TERM FINANCIAL NEEDS : The time period here is exceeding one year but not exceeding 5 years. They may include expenses on modernization of plant and machinery or introduction of a new product, distribution or an advertisement campaign. SHORT TERM FINANCIAL NEEDS : Financial Needs dealing with financing the current assets such as stock, debaters, cash etc comes under this category. The main purpose of short term financing is to meet or finance the day.	Management of funds is a critical aspect of financial management. Financial Management is the use of economic resources namely capital finds. The Scope and importance of financial management is increasing continuously. Financial Management is related with the issues involved in raising of funds, administration of funds and moving them in a business in the most optimum manner. The approach to the scope of financial management is divided into two broad groups. (1) Traditional Approach (2) Modern Approach **TRADITIONAL APPROACH** It is developed in 1906 which is Early Stage when Scientific Management developed. It is Restricted to raising of funds. In this approach "Finance is considered as an Ad hoc and occasional functions required at start up" This approach involves : (1) Arrangement of funds from financial institute (2) Arrangement of funds through instrument like share, bond There is no emphasis on allocation of funds, decision making It is kind of Narrow approach **MODEN APPROACH** It is developed during 1955 to 1957. It is Conceptual and analytical framework for financial decision making. It covers both acquisition of funds as well as their allocation It is approach in Broader sense It involves : (1) Importance of use of debts (2) Profitability and Risk Complexion.
Role of Finance Manager	**Objectives of Finance Management**
The main objective of the Finance Manager is to manage funds in such a way so that their optimum utilization and their procurement are properly balanced. (1) FINANCIAL FORECASTING : The first and foremost functions of financial management is to forecast financial needs of the concern. In estimating the financial requirements, help of various budget, profit and loss account and Balance sheet is needed. (2) ESTABLISHING ASSET MANAGEMENT POLICIES : In order to estimate and arrange for cash requirement of an enterprise, it is very necessary to decide how much cash will be invested in non-cash assets. (3) ALLOCATION OF NET PROFIT : How to allocate the net profit of the concern is an important decision for the financial manager. (4) CASH FLOWS AND REQUIREMENTS : It is the prime responsibility of the financial manager to see that an adequate supply of cash is available at proper time for smooth running of the business. (5) DECIDING UPON BOROOWING POLICY : Personal resources are limited and hence funds are arranged by borrowing money either from commercial bank or other financial institute. (6) CHECKING UPON FINANCIAL PERFORMANCE : The Financial manager is under an obligation to check the financial performance of the funds invested in the business. It requires retrospective analysis of the operating period to evaluate the efficiency of financial planning.	Simply put, the objective of financial management is to maximize the value of the firm. And while we can state this objective simply, it is much more complex than that. (1) PROFIT MAXIMIZATION – Maximization of Profit is main objectives of a business enterprise. Profit maximization aims at improving profitability, maintaining Stability and reducing losses and inefficiencies. Profit maximization has to be attempted with a realization of risks involved. A positive relationship exists between risk and profits. So both risk and profit objectives should be balanced. (2) WEALTH MAXIMIZATION – The objective of a firm is to maximize value or wealth. Wealth maximization decision is also known as value maximization. Value is represented by the market price of the ordinary share of the company. Wealth maximization is creation of wealth, property and assets over a period of time thus if profit maximization is aimed after taking care of its limitation (3) RETURN MAXIMIZATION – The objective of financial management is to safeguard the Economic interest of the person who are directly and indirectly connected with company i.e shareholders, creditors and employees. All Such persons must get the maximum return for their contributions. But this is possible only when the company earns higher profits or sufficient profits to discharge its obligation to them. Therefore, the goal of maximization of returns and profit maximization are inter - related

Functions of Financial Management	Sources of Finance
ESTIMATION OF CAPITAL REQUIREMENTS : A finance manager has to make estimation with regards to capital requirements of the company. This will depend upon expected costs and profits and future programmes and policies of a concern **DETERMINATION OF CAPITAL COMPOSITION** : Once the estimation have been made, the capital structure have to be decided. This involves short- term and long- term debt equity analysis. **INVESTMENT OF FUNDS** : The finance manager has to decide to allocate funds into profitable ventures so that there is safety on investment and regular returns is possible. **MANAGEMENT OF CASH** : Finance manager has to make decisions with regards to cash management. Cash is required for many purposes like payment of wages and salaries, payment of electricity and water bills, payment to creditors, meeting current liabilities, maintenance of enough stock, purchase of raw materials, etc. **FINANCIAL CONTROLS** : The finance manager has not only to plan, procure and utilize the funds but he also has to exercise control over finances. This can be done through many techniques like ratio analysis, financial forecasting, cost and profit control, etc.	Sources of finance can be classified into: (1) Internal sources (raised from within the organisation) (2) External (raised from an outside source) **INTERNAL SOURCES** : There are five internal sources of finance. This is money which comes from the owner/s own savings. It may be in the form of start up capital - used when the business is setting up It may be in the form of additional capital – perhaps used for expansion. This is a long-term source of finance • Owner's investment (start up or additional capital) • Retained profits • Sale of stock • Sale of fixed assets • Debt collection **EXTERNAL SOURCES** : There are five internal sources of finance: • Bank Loan or Overdraft • Additional Partners • Share Issue • Leasing • Hire Purchase • Mortgage • Trade Credit • Government Grants
Significance of Financial Planning	**Relationship of Finance Dept. with Other Dept.**
Financial Planning is the process of estimating the capital required and determining it's competition. It is the process of framing financial policies in relation to procurement, investment and administration of funds of an enterprise. **IMPORTANCE OF FINANCIAL PLANNING** Financial Planning is process of framing objectives, policies, procedures, programmes and budgets regarding the financial activities of a concern. This ensures effective and adequate financial and investment policies. The importance can be outlined as- Adequate funds have to be ensured. Financial Planning helps in ensuring a reasonable balance between outflow and inflow of funds so that stability is maintained. Financial Planning ensures that the suppliers of funds are easily investing in companies which exercise financial planning. Financial Planning helps in making growth and expansion programmes which helps in long-run survival of the company. Financial Planning reduces uncertainties with regards to changing market trends which can be faced easily through enough funds. Financial Planning helps in reducing the uncertainties which can be a hindrance to growth of the company. This helps in ensuring stability and profitability in concern.	**RELATIONSHIP OF FINANCE WITH PRODUCTION** : Production department's main duty is to produce the goods. For producing goods, it need raw material, labor and other expenses. For paying all expenses, production department needs money and funds which will be fulfilled by finance department. Finance department checks the budget of production dept. and allow funds for production. **RELATIONSHIP OF FINANCE WITH MARKETING** : Marketing department's main duty is to sell maximum goods and satisfy the consumers. Its product's input cost will decrease if all products are sold by marketers of company. For developing the product, promotion activities and distribution activities of marketing department need some money for paying salesman, advertising budget and other promotional expenses. **RELATIONSHIP OF FINANCE WITH PERSONNEL** : Personnel is that science which manages the employees of company and finance is that science which manage the money. If personnel department and finance department work together with co-operation both department can satisfy the objectives of company. **EXTRA : FINANCIAL CONTROL AND REGULATORY BODIES** (1) Internal Audit (2) Budget as Control technique Budget is a financial quantitative statement, prepared and approved prior to a defined period of time. There are different types of budgets like Operating budgets, Sales budgets, Production budgets, Material/Purchase Budget, Labour Budget or Cash Budget.

Unit - 8 : Production Management

Product , Production & Production Management	Objectives and Benefits of Production Management
PRODUCT : A good idea, method, information or service that is the end result of a process is called a product. A product can be defined as a bundle of tangible (actual good) and intangible attributes (benfits, discount, service, warranty) that a seller offer to a buyer for purchase, **PRODUCTION** converts raw materials into well finished useful goods. Production uses resources to create a good and service that is suitable for use or exchange in a market economy. The process and method to transform tangible inputs (raw material, semi-finished goods) and intangible inputs (ideas, information and knowledge) into well finished goods and service. **PRODUCTION MANAGEMENT :** Production management deals with decision making related to production process so that resulting goods or services are produced according to specification. Production Management converts input into the outputs. Production management involves decision making regarding the production of goods and service at a minimum cost. It is concerned with the manufacturing industry. Production Management is administrative discipline which converts inputs into outputs.	**OBJECTIVES :** The main objective of the production management is 'to produce goods or service of right quality and quantity at the right time and right manufacturing cost. 1) Right Quality : The quality of product is established based upon the user's needs. The right quality is not necessarily best quality. 2) Right Quantity : The manufacturing organization should produce the products in right number. 3) Right Time : Timeliness of delivery is one of the important aspect to judge the effectiveness of production system. 4) Right Manufacturing cost : Manufacturing costs are established before the product is actually manufactured. **Benefits of Production Management :** 1) More effective utilization of scarce human and material resources 2) Lower level of work in process inventory 3) Better responsiveness to customer needs 4) Better Procurement of inputs 5) On Schedule deliveries 6) Better quality control 7) Improved work environment

Plant Location and Factor affecting Plant Location	

Plant Location is an important decision which decides the fate of the business. In the past, much importance was not given to the selection of appropriate location but now it is scientific and systematic process. The selection of location is an important activity for the success of business. A good location may reduce the cost of production and distribution.
 	
The factor affecting selection of a factory can be studied in the following three stages :
   (1) Selection of the region
   (2) Selection of the locality
   (3) Selection of actual site
 	
Generally availability of raw material, vicinity of the market, labour supply, climate conditions etc are some of the major considerations in selecting the region. After selecting the region the specific locality within the region is considered.
 	
Factors must be considered while selecting the location of factory :
(1) AVAILABILITY OF RAW MATERIAL : If possible, the site selected should be near the source of raw material so that the cost of transportation can be minimized. If raw material are heavy and bulky, it becomes essential to select a site near to the source of raw material. For example, most of the iron and steel industries are situated in Orissa and Bihar.
 	
(2) MARKET : The cost of transporting finished goods, advertising and distribution etc will be greatly reduced if the factory is located near the market
 	
(3) AVAILABILITY OF LABOUR : Workers and Skilled Labour should be available at your place of plant location. Glass and Bangle industry in Ferozabad and Silk Saree at Kanziwaram, Cracker at Shivakashi are mainly due to highly skilled labour available at place.
	(4) TRANSPORT AND COMMUNICATION : Transport facilities are needed for transporting raw materials, parts and finished goods. Generally industries should be near the railway station, highway or port areas. Railways are cheaper but involve delay. Road transport is quick, it is convenient for door to door service. Communication facilities like mail, telephone, mobile signal must be adequate.
	
	(4) AVAILABILITY OF POWER AND FUEL : Coal, electricity, oil and natural gas are important sources of power in the industries. The availability of reliable and cheap power supply is an important factor in the location of electro-chemical industries, glass, pulp and paper industries.
	
	(5) CLIMATE CONDITIONS : Climate condition largely affect certain production and also the efficiency of the employees. For example textile mills require moist climate that is why most of textile mills are situated at Bombay and Ahemdabad. For agro based industries like tea and coffee or rubber plantations, climate conditions play a decisive role in the selection of site.
	
	(6) AVAILABILITY OF WATER : Water is used in industries for processing. Water is also required for drinking and sanitary purpose because industries consists of many workers and laborer. Water should be in adequate quantity and should be proper quality.
	
	(7) FINANCIAL AND OTHER AIDS : For the development of backward regions, Government provide certain facility and subsidy, concession etc,
	
	(8) BUSINESS AND COMMERCIAL FACILITIES : For day to day management of finance , banking services are considered highly desirable.

Types of Plant Layout

Plant Layout can be defined as an overall arrangement of industrial facilities including personnel equipment, storage space, material handling equipment and all other supporting services in an existing or proposed plants. A Plant Layout is an arrangement of facilities and services in the plant. Plant Layout is planning and arrangement of 4M's – Men, Material, Machinery and Method for achieving coordination

Plant layout refers to the arrangement of physical facilities such as machines, equipment, tools, furniture etc. in well arranged manner to get quickest flow of material at the lowest cost and with the least amount of handling in processing the product from the receipt of raw material to the delivery of the final product

IMPORTANCE :
A Good Layout is one which allows materials to move rapidly and directly for processing. This reduces transport, handling, clerical and other costs down per unit and reduces idle machine and idle labor time.

OBJECTIVES
- Proper and efficient utilization of available floor space.
- Reduce material handling costs
- Provide ease of supervision and control.
- Allow easy maintenance of machines and plant.
- Worker Convenience and Job Satisfaction
- Removal of bottlenecks
- Integrate the production centres
- Minimum waste of time

FACTORS AFFECTING PLANT LOCATION
Management Policy
Manufacturing Process
Nature of Product
Type of Equipment and Machines
Type of Building
Availability of Total Floor Area
Arrangement of Material Handling equipment

TYPES OF PLANT LAYOUT :
(1) PROCESS LAYOUT / FUNCTIONAL LAYOUT/ JOB LOT LAYOUT
(2) PRODUCT LAYOUT/LINE LAYOUT
(3) MIXED LAYOUT
(4) STATIC LAYOUT

(1) PROCESS LAYOUT / FUNCTIONAL LAYOUT

All machines performing similar type of operations are grouped at one location in the process layout. All Lathe, milling machines, cutting machines are in same section. The process dominates product. Process Layout is more suitable for job order industries like steel fabrication, hosiery, printing etc   The primary requirement in process layout is flexibility.

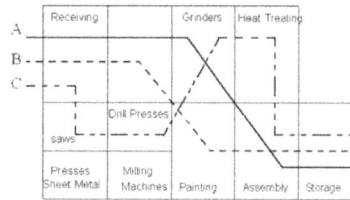

MERITS :
- Eliminates the duplication of machines
- Specialized Supervision is possible
- Individual Rate Scheme is possible.

DEMERITS :
- The problem of bottleneck and waiting
- Material handling cost increases
- Inspection & Supervision cost increases

Types of Plant Layout

(2) PRODUCT OR LINE LAYOUT :

In this type, machines and auxiliary are arranged in line according to the sequence of operations to be perfomed on the work.
The raw material enters in the line at one end, the operations are carried out in a smooth flow and the finished product is delivered at the other end.

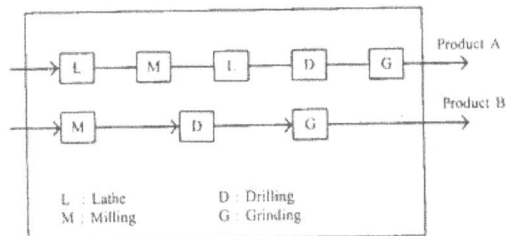

L : Lathe   D : Drilling
M : Milling   G : Grinding

MERITS :
- Reduced Material Handling
- Speedier Movements of Materials
- Maximum utilization of machine
- Supervision costs reduced
- Maximum use of space

DEMERITS :
- Duplication of Machines and Equipment
- Break Down in any machine in the line interrupts entire process
- Specialized supervision is not possible
- Since it is joint efforts , it is difficult to implement individual rate sheme.

(3) MIXED OR COMBINED LAYOUT :

- Pure Process or Pure Layout are rare. The combination of these is very commonly used in industry. The combined layout unites the benefits of process and product layout.

- Production shops may be arranged by process layout, while the assembly is arranged by product layout.

(4) STATIC OR FIXED LAYOUT

- When work piece is very big or too heavy to move from one position to the other and is fixed in one place. The machine and men move with respect to the work to perform the required operation.

- Construction work, Ship Building, Tanks, Air Craft

HOW TO UNDERSTAND EASILY

Suppose mobile manufacturing company makes mobile by assembling battery, cover, processor and packing in box. Suppose battery are fixed in mobile body in one room, then entire item shift to another room to fix processor and in the last room , mobile with accessories are packed. That is called Process Layout.

The Same mobile is produced by assembling batter,cover,processor in one room and in line format. It is called Product / Line Layout.

Break Even Analysis

Simple speaking , Break Even Point is a point where there is no loss or no profit condition. Break Even Analysis is a techniques that helps decision makers understand the relationship among sales volume, costs and revenue in any organization. Break Even Analysis is graphical method of analyzing. It is also known as cost volume profit (CVP) analysis. In this method break even point, the level of sales volume to which total revenues equal total costs is determined. Break Even Analysis can be carried out in two ways : (1) Algebraic Method (2) Graphical Method

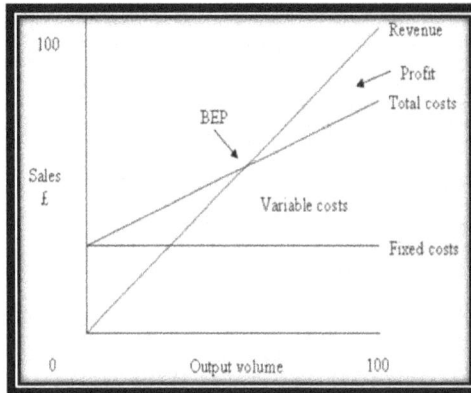

ASSUMPTIONS IN BREAK EVEN ANALYSIS
(1) The total cost of production can be divided into two categories (a) Fixed Cost (b) Variable cost
(2) Fixed cost remain costant i.e it is independent of quantity produced and include executive salaries, rent of building, pant and equipment
(3) The variable cost varies directly and proportionately with the volume of production If V = variable cost per unit and Q is the quantity produced variable cost = V X Q
(4) The Selling Price does change with change in the volume of sales. If P is the selling price per unit. The Total Sales income = P X Q
(5) The firm deals with only one product or the sales mxl remains unchanged
(6) Productivity per worker and efficiency of plan etc., remains mostly unchanged

APPLICATION OF BREAK EVEN ANALYSIS

(1) Break Even Analysis is useful in determining optimum level of output
(2) To determine minimum cost for a given level of output
(3) To determine impact of changes in cost or selling price on break even point
(4) It is useful in choosing a product mix
(5) It is useful in budgeting and profit planning
(6) It is a decision making tool in the hand of management

LIMITATIONS OF BREAK EVEN ANALYSIS

(1) The Analysis is based on fixed costs, variable costs and total revenue. Any change in one variable affects break even point.
(2) Multiple charts are to be produced in case of multi-product firm.
(3) The break even chart is based on fixed cost concept and hence holds good for a short period.
(4) Break even analysis is not suitable under fluctuating business environment.

TYPES OF PRODUCTION SYSTEM	COMPUTER ASSIGNED LAYOUT PLANNING
In general there are three types of production systems, these are stated below (1) Job Production (2) Batch Production (3) Continuous Production	Computer can be very much effectively used in planning. Number of layout modeling software are available for layout planning.
(1) Job Production : In this system Products are manufactured to meet the requirements of a specific order. The quality involved is small and the manufacturing of the product will take place as per the specifications given by the customer.	(1) CORELAP – First Constructive algorithm that was developed and computerized by Lee and More
	(2) CRAFT – Populare and widely used for layout planning
(2) Batch Production : Batch Production is the manufacture of number of identical products either to meet the specific order or to satisfy the demand.	(3) BLOCPLAN – is an interactive program which can develop a single story or multistory layout
	(4) FactoryCAD - It customizes AutoCAD
(3) Continuous Production system is the specialized manufacture of identical products on which the machinery and equipment is fully engaged. The continuous production is normally associated with large quantities and with high rate of demand. and.	(6) FactoryPLAN – is a qualitative analysis tool.
	(7) FactoryFLOW – us

ALL IN ONE SUM

An ABC Co. Ltd. is producing XYZ item with selling cost Rs. 22 per unit, Variable cost Rs. 20 per unit and Fixed Cost : Rs. 5000

Calculate
  (1) BEP in Units
  (2) BEP in Rs.
  (3) Profit at Current Level (Quantity / Sales in 10000 Units)
  (4) Margin of Safety if quantity/Sales is 10000 Units
  (5) P/V Ratio
  (6) BEP using P/V Ratio
  (7) If profit is Rs.10000 then calculate no. of units (Quantity//Sales) which is to be produced
  (8) If Quantity /Sales is 50000 Units then calculate profit
  (9) Find out sales turnover if desired profit is Rs. 60000

BEP in UNITS = $\dfrac{\text{Total Fixed Cost}}{\text{Selling Price} - \text{Variable cost per unit}}$ = $\dfrac{5000}{22 - 20}$ = 2500

BEP IN RUPEES = $\dfrac{\text{Total Fixed Cost}}{\text{Selling Price} - \text{Variable Cost}}$ X Selling Price = $\dfrac{5000}{22 - 20}$ = Rs. 55000

Profit at current level = Total Contribution - Fixed Cost

Total Contribution = (Selling Cost – Variable Cost) X Number of Units Sold
                   = (22 -20) X 10000
                   = 20000 Rs.

Profit = 20000 – 5000 Rs.
       = Rs. 15000

Margin of Safety = Current Sales – BEP Sales
                 = 10000 X SP – 55000 Rupees
                 = 220000 – 55000
                 = 165000

P/V Ratio = Profit / Volume Ratio = SC – VC / SC = 22 – 20 / 22 X 100 = 9.09 %

BEP using P/V Ratio = Fixed cost / P/V Ratio = 5000/9 *100 = 55555

Profit = Sales Price X Quantity - Fixed Cost - Variable Cost X Quantity   (SC XQ - [FC + VCXQ])
10000 = 22Q – 5000 – 20 Q
15000 = 2Q
Quantity = 7500 Units

Profit = Sales Price X Quantity - Fixed Cost - Variable Cost X Quantity
       = 22X50000 – 5000 – 20X50000
       = 9500 Rs.

Sales Turnover = $\dfrac{\text{Total Fixed Cost} + \text{Desired Profit}}{\text{Selling Price} - \text{Variable cost per unit}}$ = $\dfrac{5000 + 60000}{22 - 20}$ = 64998 Rs.

Different SUM : The P/V Ratio of Matrix is 40 % and margin of Safety is 30 %. You are required to count BEP and Net profit if the sales volume is Rs. 14000

PV Ratio = 40 % = 0.4
Margin of Safety = 30 % = 0.3
Sales Volume = Rs. 14000

BEP = Sales Volume – Margin of Safet = 14000 – (30% 14000) = 14000 – 4200 = 9800 Rs.

Net Profit = Margin of Safety X PV Ratio = 4200 X 0.4 = Rs. 1680

Unit - 9 : Human Resource Management

Human Resource Management	Objectives & Functions of HRM
Human Resources Management means employing people, developing their resources, utilizing, maintaining and compensating their services in tune with the job and organizational requirement. HRM is a process that consists of four functions - acquiring, developing, motivating and retaining human resources. The basic task of HRM is the selection of the right person for the right job at the right time to carry out the activities of an organization in the most efficient way.	**OBJECTIVES** (1) To act as a liaison between top management and employees (2) To enable management to achieve organizational objectives (3) To utilize the manpower to its full capacity and potential (4) To create environment in which the creativity of employees will be rise. (5) To get right people in the right place at the right time (6) To ensure that staff moves in the right direction (7) To maintain healthy and safe working environment.
The activities of HR include <ul><li>Human Resource Planning</li><li>Job Analysis and Job Design</li><li>Recruitment and Selection</li><li>Orientation and Placements</li><li>Training and Developments</li><li>Performance Appraisal</li><li>Job Evaluation</li><li>Employee and Executive Remuneration</li><li>Motivation and Communication</li><li>Welfare</li><li>Safety and Health</li><li>Industrial Relations</li></ul>	**FUNCTIONS OF HRM** (1) <u>FORMULATING HRM STRATEGY</u> : It deals with long term development. (2) <u>RESTRUCTURING OF ORGANIZATION</u> : Helping organization in restructuring of organizations. (3) <u>TRAINING AND DEVELOPMENT</u> : By this, Company's mission and values are identified. (4) <u>RESOURCING</u> : Resourcing is acquiring human resources to the changing requirements of the organization. (5) <u>HUMAN RESOURCE PLANNING</u> : Human Resource planning uses demand and supply forecasting techniques to determine the future workforce requirements of the company. (6) <u>Compensation and Reward</u> : Compensation determines salary and wages.
HRM is all about learning the art of understanding people. HRM is concerned with policies and practices that ensure the best use of human resources. Human resources alone can produce an output larger than the input.	*The activities of HR include Human Resource Planning, Job Analysis and Job Design, Recruitment and Selection, Orientation and Placements, Training and Developments ,Performance Appraisal, Job Evaluation, Employee and Executive Remuneration, Welfare, Safety and Health*

Sources of Recruitment

Recruitment is a process of searching eligible candidates from various sources and attracting them to apply for the vacant job. There are two types of sources of recruitment : (1) Internal (2) External ### INTERNAL SOURCE OF RECRUITMENT Internal sources refer to recruiting known persons who are familiar with culture, policies and expectation of the organization. (1) <u>TEMPORARY WORKERS</u> : Workers who joined as trainee on a nominal stipend will be recruited as regular employee. (2) <u>PROMOTIONS</u> : Positions vacant in higher ranks can be filled up by suitable employees from the lower levels. (3) <u>TRANSFERS</u> : A transfer deals with the shifting of an employee from one job to another without special reference to change in responsibility or compensation. <u>MERITS</u> (1) Quickest and Cheapest Method (2) Economical and Convenient to the business firm (3) No direction and induction process required (4) Help in boosting employee morale (5) Motivates other employees to work better <u>DEMERITS</u> : (1) Current employees may not be aware of the latest technology and trends in the market (2) Promotion based on seniority may de-motivate a meritorious candidate. (3) It limits the choice to few employees (4) It may become bias (5) May create frustration for candidate who are not selected.	**EXTERNAL SOURCE OF RECRUITMENT** External sources attract outsiders to a chance of entry in the company. (1) <u>RECRUITMENT AT THE FACTORY GATE</u> : It is the cheapest way and used to recruit unskilled workers to fill up casual vacancies. Most appointment done through this method are temporary. (2) <u>RECOMMENDATION OF EXISTING EMPLOYEES</u> : Those who are working in company will recommend someone form outside. A present employee will never wish to mislead company. (3) <u>JOB ADVETISEMENTS</u> : This is done by giving advertisement of vacancies in local newspapers or in professional journals. (4) <u>LABOUR CONTRACTORS</u> : When the work is of temporary nature, labour contactor is useful in completing those tasks. Housekeeping staff and Colour Painting Staff can be hired on temporary basis. (5) <u>EMPLOYMENT AGENCIES</u> : They may be public or private. They provide screening facilities. (6) <u>EDUCATIONAL AND TECHNICAL INSTITUTES</u> : Searching form educational and technical institutes is also known as campus recruitment. New fresh graduates can be hired by this technique. (7) <u>UNSOLICTIED APPLICANTS</u> : Some candidate sometimes drop application without any advertisement. They are appointed if vacancies are available. <u>MERITS</u> : Fresh talent and skill comes into the organization. New employees change the old norms and habits. They can form new policy and terms. <u>DEMERITS</u> : Outsiders are not fully aware with the policies and procedures. Problem of Sorting during Campus Inteview and Advertment will arise. Lack of time may lead to faulty selection of candidates.

Manpower Resource Planning & Process of Manpower Planning

Manpower Planning which is also called as Human Resource Planning consists of putting right number of people, right kind of people at the right place, right time, doing the right things for which they are suited for the achievement of goals of the organization. Human Resource Planning has got an important place in the arena of industrialization. Human Resource Planning has to be a systems approach and is carried out in a set procedure. The procedure is as follows:

1) Analyzing the current manpower inventory
2) Making future manpower forecasts
3) Developing employment programmes
4) Design training programmes

PROCESS OF MANPOWER RESOURCE PLANNING

(1) ANALYZING THE CURRENT MANPOWER INVENTORY - Before a manager makes forecast of future manpower, the current manpower status has to be analyzed. For this the following things have to be noted-Type of organization, Number of departments, Number and quantity of such departments, Employees in these work units

(2) MAKING FUTURE MANPOWER FORECASTS - Once the factors affecting the future manpower forecasts are known, planning can be done for the future manpower requirements in several work units.

(3) DEVELOPING EMPLOYMENT PROGRAMMES - Once the current inventory is compared with future forecasts, the employment programmes can be framed and developed accordingly, which will include recruitment, selection procedures and placement plans.

(4) DESIGN TRAINING PROGRAMMES - These will be based upon extent of diversification, expansion plans, development programmes,etc. Training programmes depend upon the extent of improvement in technology and advancement to take place. It is also done to improve upon the skills, capabilities, knowledge of the workers.

IMPORTANCE OF MANPOWER PLANNING

(1) KEY TO MANAGERIAL FUNCTIONS - The four managerial functions, i.e., planning, organizing, directing and controlling are based upon the manpower.

(2) EFFICIENT UTILIZATION - Efficient management of personnels becomes an important function in the industrialization world of today.

(3) MOTIVATION - Staffing function not only includes putting right men on right job, but it also comprises of motivational programmes

(4) BETTER HUMAN RELATIONS - Staffing function also looks after training and development of the work force which leads to co-operation and better human relations.

(5) HIGHER PRODUCTIVITY - Productivity level increases when resources are utilized in best possible manner. higher productivity is a result of minimum wastage of time, money, efforts and energies. This is possible through the staffing and it's related activities.

Recruitment vs Selection

RECRUITMENT	SELECTION
(1) It is the process of searching the candidate for a vacant job and attracting them to apply for the same.	(1) It is the process of selection of right type of candidate and offering them a job.
(2) It is a positive process.	(2) It is a negative process.
(3) Its aim is to attract more and more candidates.	(3) Its aim is to reject unsuitable candidates.
(4) It takes place before selection.	(4) It is done after recruitment.
(5) No contract can be created at this stage.	(5) Leads to a contractual agreement as this stage aims at finalizing appointment.
(6) It is an economical method	(6) It is an expensive method.
(7) Less time is required.	(7) More time is required.

Selection Tests : Types of Tests

(1) INTELLIGENCE TEST : This test aims at measuring the IQ (Intelligence quotient) of the candidate with respect to their levels of reasoning, perception, numerical ability, understanding memory, speed of thought etc.

(2) APTITUDE TEST : These tests aim at measuring some potential of a certain kind rather than acquired skill or knowledge.

(3) COMPETENCE TESTS : These test are used to test the depth of knowledge acquired in the past .

(4) INTEREST TESTS : This is to determine the preference of the candidate to accept occupation of a different kind.

(5) PERSONALITY TEST : These tests are conducted to judge the emotional balance, maturity and temperamental qualities of a person. These tests generally aim at finding out the characteristics that make up a candidates personality.

(6) GROUP or INDIVIDUAL TEST : These tests can find out leadership qualities of the candidates. The ability to work with the group is tested.

Selection Process

Selection is the process of selection of right type of candidate and offering them a job. The steps of Selection process are as follows :

(1) Employment Application Forms / Blanks : Standardized format to collect the necessary information
(2) Selection Test : This is a psychological test.
(3) Selection Interview : This is face to face conversation with the candidate to collect the required information
(4) Reference Check : This is a process of cross-checking information provided by the candidates in different stages of the selection.
(5) Physical Examination : This is a medical test to check physical requirements
(6) Job Offer : A Job offer is a formal communication form the employer.

Unit - 10 : Strategic Management

Management by Objectives (MBO)

DEFINITION : MBO is a system wherein the superior and subordinate of an organization jointly identify its common goals, define individual's responsibility in terms of expected results.

MBO gained attention because

(1) It focuses on objectives and results which a manager wants to achieve in specific time.
(2) It focuses on participative management.

The term MBO is coined by Peter Drucker in 1954 in his work "The Practice of Management"

"MBO is a result centered managerial process for the effective utilization of material, physical and human resources of the organization."

FEATURES :

MBO tries to combine long range goals of organization with short range goals. MBO's emphasis is not only on goals but also effective performance. It also focuses of the participation of employees in goal setting process.

PROCESS OF MBO

1. DEFINING ORGANIZATIONAL OBJECTIVES : : First Long rang goals are designed. Short term Goals are designed taking into account the feasibilility of achieveing the long term objectives.

2. GOALS FOR EACH SECTION : Objectives are distrivbuted for each department and section.

3. FIXING KEY RESULT AREA : KRA are arranged on a priority basis. The example of KRA are profitibilty, market standing, innovation.

4. FRANK DISCUSSION BETWEEN SUPERIOR AND SUBORDINATE: There should be frank Discussion between Superior and Subordinate for clear understanding of goals.

5. MATCHING RESOURCES WITH OBJECTIVES : You need to analyze resources, the objectives are decided on the basis of availability of resources.

6. PERIODICAL REVIEW MEETING : The superior and subordinate should hold meetings periodically.

7. APPRAISAL OF ACTIVITIES (SUBORDINATE PERFORMANCE) : This is controlling function where subordinate actual performance is measured with predetermined objective.

8. REAPPRAISAL OF OBJECTIVES : Every manager must reappraise the emphasis he gives to his various objectives.

BENEFITS

- *Manager can understand their role in organization. MBO give the criteria of performance. It helps to take corrective action.*

- *Decision is taken by the management very quickly. Because the workers knows the purpose of taking a decision and does not oppose the decision.*

- *Mangers are involved in objectives in MBO and it ensures hard work to achieve them. It provides a foundation for participative management.*

LIMITATIONS

- *MBO fails because executives do not know how MBO works, what is MBO and why is MBO necessary.*

- *It only focuses on short term objectives and doesn't consider long term objectives.*

- *MBO is rigid one. Objectives should be changed according to changed circumstance, external or internal. It is difficult to make comparative ratings of individuals because each individual goals are different from others. It is time consuming.*

REASONS FOR FAILURE :

- *Absence of a fully committed and involved top management.*

- *Top Level Management always prefer dominating attitude, don't want participative management.*

Levels of Strategy	Strategic Plan & Operational Plan
CORPORATE LEVEL STRATEGY Corporate level strategy is the highest level of strategic decision-making and covers actions dealing with the objective of the firm, acquisition and allocation of resources and coordination of strategies of various SBUs for optimal performance. Top management of the organization makes such decisions. **BUSINESS-LEVEL STRATEGY** Business-level strategy is applicable in those organizations, which have different businesses-and each business is treated as strategic business unit (SBU). The fundamental concept in SBU is to identify the discrete independent product/market segments served by an organization. Since each product/market segment has a distinct environment, a SBU is created for each such segment. For example, Reliance Industries Limited operates in textile fabrics, yarns, fibers, and a variety of petrochemical products. For each product group, the nature of market in terms of customers, competition, and marketing channel differs. **FUNCTIONAL STRATEGY** Functional strategy, as is suggested by the title, relates to a single functional operation and the activities involved therein. Functional strategy deals with relatively restricted plan providing objectives for specific function. For example, marketing strategy, a functional strategy, can be subdivided into promotion, sales, distribution, pricing strategies with each sub function strategy contributing to functional strategy. Reliance Company's main strategy is called Corporate Level Strategy. Reliance's different Businesses like Textile, Fabric, Energy as individual unit have different kind of Business Level Strategy. In each Units of Reliance, they have different departments like Marketing, Finance, Production. These departments have Functional strategy.	**STRATEGIC PLAN :** A Strategic Plan is concerned with building a full long range plan. It is simply a document that summarize in ten pages of written text. It is process of deciding objectives. It asks certain question : (1) Why a business exits ? (2) How will it try to achieve its objectives ? A Strategic Plan looks at long duration like ten years or twenty years. A Strategic Plan is the process of deciding main and long range objectives. **OPERATIONAL PLAN :** An Operational Plan is a description of how the work will be done. It focuses on the method of flow of work from input to output. An Operational Plan is a subset of strategic plan. An Operational Plan is a short term plan. Suppose, An Strategic plan will cover 10 years then 10 years individual operational plan will try to achieve objective of 10 years' strategic plan. It is the process of deciding method to achieve long range objectives. Suppose. We want to open one pizza food chain & want to make it international brand. For that, we have 10 year strategic plan. But what to add as ingredient & other short term plans falls into the category of operational plan. One another example is like this : If any cricket team wants to win next world cup after loosing world cup, they will decide one strategic plan. This strategic plan is a long range plan of 4 years. Now to achieve that objectives, we need to choose a method. Team should win small tournaments. Team should take part in workshop etc. These kind of small plans which is helpful in achieving main objectives is called Operational Plan.
The word Strategy is derived from the ancient Greek Word "Strategia" which means the art and science of directing Military faces. Strategic is a systematic plan of action. Strategy is the unified, comprehensive and integrated plan which is designed to achieve basic objectives of the enterprise through proper implementation process.	

www.ingramcontent.com/pod-product-compliance
Lightning Source LLC
Chambersburg PA
CBHW082113210326
41599CB00033B/6690